All the Tim
the world

An anthology of prose
and verse celebrating
grandparenthood

Edited by Elizabeth Cairns

B O O K S

To my grandchildren
Daniel, Rosa, Giulio and Max

© Collection, Introduction and
Notes Elizabeth Cairns 1995

Published by Age Concern England
1268 London Road, London SW16 4ER

Design, typesetting and production
Eugenie Dodd Typographics

Copy preparation Vinnette Marshall

Printed and bound in Great Britain
by Bell & Bain Ltd, Glasgow

A catalogue record for this book is
available from the British Library.

ISBN 0–86242–177–2

Front cover: BAL37616 Grandmother Reading to Children
by Cassatt, Mary (1844–1926) Private Collection,
New York/Bridgeman Art Library, London

Contents

Introduction

*'The entrance requirements for grampahood are compara-
tively mild/You only have to live till your child has had a
child.'*   OGDEN NASH

An easy prescription? In the twentieth century, perhaps.
But until modern times grandparenthood was a privileged
state. The chances of either living long enough to have
grandchildren or, if you did, of the grandchildren surviving,
were low.

Until the 1800s infant mortality in Europe was 20 times
higher than it is today. It was not until the end of the eighteenth century that people had a more than one-in-two
chance of living to be old enough to take that first necessary
step along the road to grandparenthood – having children
themselves. These bleak facts were the context for what has
been described as the 'emotional blankness' of infancy
in earlier times, when babies and young children were left to
survive or die without great concern during their first five
or six years.

It is hard to gauge the calibre of this blankness. Certainly,
a great silence seems to reign for centuries on the subject of
grandchildren. Where they are mentioned they tend to be
seen as instruments for securing property or described with
studied detachment. Witness Cicero, writing in 49 BC to tell
his best friend Atticus of the birth of his first grandchild:
'My dear Tullia had a baby on May 19, a seven months' boy.
She had a good delivery, for which I am thankful; but as for
the child, it is a weakling.' The tone of this last phrase suggests he is steeling himself against the inevitable – what were

the chances of a premature baby surviving then? Emotional blankness may have been simply a mask for pain.

The sadness and sense of loss show through the mask, however. Not everyone could be as aloofly succinct as Montaigne when he wrote that his own children 'all died at nurse except Leanor, my one daughter'. We read of a seventeenth-century Marquess of Halifax whose 'heart was set on raising his family. But though he made a vast estate for them, he buried two of his sons himself, and almost all his grandchildren.' More poignantly, his contemporary Sir William Temple was 'wounded to the Heart by Grief, upon the many losses of his children and friends'.

Because it is so rare an example, I have put the account of a particularly touching seventeenth-century grandparent-grandchild relationship at the beginning of this collection: the description of Dr Bentley by his grandson Richard Cumberland. Dr Bentley's tolerant affection and respect for the young boy is the more remarkable, given the highly developed sense of their role as mentors, if not absolute arbiters, that most grandparents seem to have had in those days. Lady Mary Wortley Montagu's letter to her daughter is an example of what today we might think of as bossy grand-mothering – though would not her exhortations about encouraging children to read be as relevant in the telly-watching twentieth century as in the illiterate eighteenth? But the prize for grandparental interference must go to Queen Victoria, with her stream of advice to her motherless granddaughter, Princess Victoria of Hesse.

Viewed from the standpoint of the late twentieth century, this concentration on advice as opposed to simple love and acceptance of the grandchild for what he or she is must, one feels, have been endlessly irritating to its recipients. In the context of the times, however, it was perfectly under-standable. This compulsion to advise, to interfere, was surely rooted in fear for the child's survival. The background to Queen Victoria's letters was the death not only of the young princess's mother from diphtheria but of her younger sister too. Lady Mary Wortley Montagu herself had barely survived smallpox, which left her disfigured for life: she was in fact the first person to introduce inoculation into this country, using it for her own son in 1717 after importing the doctor from Turkey for the purpose. Grandparental energies were devoted, first and foremost, to ensuring the survival of their descendants; secondly, to seeing that they were equipped for the world they would, if they were lucky, grow up in.

For a twentieth-century equivalent of this we have to look to cultures outside Europe. In the advice to his grandson of Chief Tom Sayachapis, a Nuuchah-nulth Indian from north-west Canada, one can see the same unquestioned awareness of the duty of the grandparent to pass on basic survival skills. Queen Victoria may have been more concerned with marriage and deportment than canoes or hospitality, but the same motive inspired them both. A recent article in *Scientific American* makes this interesting observation: 'Among all mammals our [human] infants are the most poorly equipped by themselves. Perhaps we need not only parents but grandparents too to care for us and to pass on special survival tips.'

The obverse side of this grandparental obligation to advise was the authority the office invested its holders with: the word of a grandfather (or grandmother) was law. Thus a fifteenth-century directive from a father to a son about to start employment with the Bishop of Norwich: 'You shall in all Things reverence, honour and obey my Ld Bp of Norwich, as you would any of your Parents, esteeminge whatsoever He shall tell or Command you, as if your Grandmother, your Mother, or myself should say it.' What a distant world that seems! However, if we move across to yet another continent today we find something not dissimilar. Nisa, the young girl in the extract about the !Kung people of the Kalahari Desert, has to obey parents and grandmother at the risk of being beaten if she does not; but in her case she cleverly manages to play them off against each other.

History does not relate whether the fifteenth-century squire did that too. But obedience was clearly beginning to wear thin by the time John Keats went with his siblings to be brought up by their grandmother, Mrs Jennings, in the early 1800s: he put minnows and tittlebats from the local brook into his grandmama's washing tub, but received no beating. At about the same time Jane Austen gives us a telling glimpse of a discussion between Emma and her father on how his grandchildren (her nephews) should be treated. Mr Woodhouse has been complaining about the boys' father (his son-in-law):

> '[He] tosses them up to the ceiling in a very frightful way.'
> [Emma] 'But they like it Papa; there is nothing they like so much . . .'
> 'Well, I cannot understand it.'
> 'That is the case with us all, Papa. One half of the world cannot understand the pleasures of the other half.'

Emma has put her finger on it. Midway between generations – one could almost say midway between ages – she understands that little Henry and John love being thrown in the air; and their grandfather's disapproval will make no difference whatsoever.

Times were changing; children and their grandparents (particularly among the better fed) were beginning to live longer. Instead of the age-old authority–obedience formula a tendency to idealise was beginning to creep in, on both sides, as if to compensate for all those centuries of mourning and neglect. And it continued through the nineteenth century. The excerpts from Proust and Gorky both in their very different ways offer almost religious testimony to what the writers see as the redemptive power of a grandmother's love; while the passage from Dickens' *Old Curiosity Shop* shows the same, but with a grandfather and grandchild in a curious reversal of roles. 'I am the child, and she the grown person,' says the old man of Little Nell, his granddaughter. This book, Dickens said, bound his reading public to him closer than any other that he wrote. It clearly touched a deep nerve in Victorian society.

In *Hard Times* Dickens paints a very different picture of grandparenting, with his thumb-nail sketch of Mr Bounderby's grandmother (one might have expected that unpleasant character to have chequered antecedents):

> *My grandmother was the wickedest and worst old woman that ever lived. If I got a little pair of shoes by any chance, she would take 'em off and sell 'em for drink. Why, I have known that grandmother of mine lie in her bed and drink fourteen glasses of liquor before breakfast . . . She kept a chandler's shop . . . and kept me in an egg box. That was the cot of my infancy; an old egg-box.*

A breath of fresh air after Little Nell? Maybe. But what was the reality? The answer, I think, depended on what part of society you belonged to; and it was the same everywhere. Russia could produce Tolstoy's distant, elegant grandmama, Gorky's loving peasant granny and Isaac Babel's – obsessive, canny, tough – all within 50 years of each other. The description of Mr Bounderby's grandmother may not have been exaggerated by Dickens. One only has to think of Gustava Doré's engravings of life in the slums of London in the 1870s to feel its authenticity. The Bounderby granny's natural heir is perhaps Kathleen Dayus' grandmother, crashing like a rogue elephant into her son's cramped household in the Birmingham of the 1900s.

But a certain awe survives: whatever changes in class or social setting, children still seem to treat their grandparents as something special, different from the rest of humanity, even today. This message comes across again and again. In some cases it is only to be expected. In Gwen Raverat's account of her grandfather, Charles Darwin, she tells us: 'We always felt embarrassed if our grandfather were mentioned, just as we did if God were spoken of. In fact, he was obviously in the same category as God and Father Christmas.' The rest of us cannot hope to be up there on the platform with Father Christmas, but we undoubtedly have a place, if only on the bottom steps of a nearby podium.

Perhaps the key to this is that we grandparents are not parents; we are both a little less than parents and a little more. Less concerned with the here and now (the uneaten sprouts, the lost sock, the sudden squabble), more concerned with . . . fun? 'Fun' of course is a modern concept, born of leisure and longevity – both of which, compared with our forebears, we have. We can forget our policeman role of the past; yet does something of it still remain in the consciousness of our charges, or perhaps even in our own manner? If not, then why is it that our grandchildren tend to behave so much better with us than with the rest of their families, particularly their parents?

Perhaps, indeed, race memories of the struggle for survival in earlier ages have left their mark and metamorphosed the grandparent into something of a magic figure in the deepest layers of our subconscious. Certainly in some cultures less divorced from their roots than ours the grandparental image has been endowed with superhuman power: among Lakota (Sioux) Indians 'Grandfather' is the name for the rock used as altar and for solemn oath-taking. In parts of rural Europe up until the 1920s the last sheaf of corn was called 'the Grandmother', with the harvesters competing for it and the one who got it sure to marry within the year. . . .

Superhuman totem, fertility symbol? This seems a far cry from our grandparental world today. However, even in our materialist culture one mythological grandparent still survives, and she is known to us all: the grandmother who made her granddaughter a little red cloak and then got herself eaten by a wolf (rather an exhibition of lack of potency than the reverse, it might be argued).

However, to me the interesting thing about that story is that while the huntsman, arriving at the end, immediately spots that the figure in the bed is a wolf, Little Red-Cap fails to do this even when she is very close and already alerted to her grandmother's changed appearance. Either she is very trusting or very dumb – or could it be that she sees her grandmother as something of a wolf figure already?

A wolf grandmother appears again in the short excerpt from Sylvia Townsend-Warner's story, and there are sug-gestions of her in other pieces too: Salim Hakim's grandmother, with her black rosary (was it not 'the work of the devil himself'?), David Malouf's grandmother with her winding skeins of wool. Isn't there an element of fear in all of these? Some of us may be able to remember it from our own long ago grandchildhood. It seems to me that a spectrum of emotions, from love through awe to – sometimes – fear, is perfectly natural to the young in their relations with the old, particularly their grandparents who, after all, have known so much about them and for so very long; from their very beginning, in fact.

J B Priestley, in an article on 'Growing Old', identified 'magic' as an element in this relationship; he saw children and their grandparents as part of a conspiracy that excludes the ages in between. Sevens and 75-year-olds, he said, 'are both closer to the world of magic and mythology than all the busier people between those ages'. This is magic as enchantment, the opposite of fear, 'close to wonder and far from worry, often common to childhood and old age'. Just such benign enchantment colours 'The Fragrance of Herbs', by Jayabrato Chatterjee, where a grandfather and grandson talk about the most solemn question of all – death – with the fearlessness and ease of profound mutual love.

'Living with many traditional families over the years, I have experienced the depth of the bond between children and their grandparents. It is clearly a natural relationship, with a very different dimension from that between parent and child.' Thus the verdict of Helena Norberg-Hodge, whose description of a Ladakhi grandparent I have included here. The world she describes is a long way from our own society. Nevertheless, as a grandparent, I can relate to her statement about the 'naturalness' of the relationship and its depths. This does not mean to say that it is not also daunting; both the Glazer story and the excerpt from Nell Dunn bear witness to this. But it is because of its very depths that we are daunted, when we contemplate what we are letting ourselves in for.

What are we taking on? In practical terms, anything from babysitting to knitting, carpentry, cakemaking . . . But it's not the practical side that daunts, it's the emotional blank cheque, or rather standing order, we're poised to sign – for limitless love, for the rest of our lives. And what do we get in return?

I would say: a heightened sense of time's continuum, of our place on it and of our individual entity as one link in its long chain. For our grandchildren, we are their link with the past, a past they may not want to know about yet, but one day will, while they are our link to the future; their future, not ours, but one that by a process of osmosis becomes ours through them. Shakespeare, in his second sonnet, putting the argument for having children, in an age when people were old at 40, could have been making the case for grand-children when he wrote: 'This were to be new made when thou art old/And see thy blood warm when thou feel'st it cold.'

This anthology ends with the poem by Po Chü-I. I have placed it there not simply because of its title, 'Last Poem', but because the scene it describes is the mirror image of the picture on the cover of this book of a grandmother reading to her grandchildren, with this difference: the child is read-ing to the grandparent. A thousand years separate picture and poem. Po Chü-I, who lived in the ninth century and wrote upwards of 3,000 poems, took comfort from the knowledge that these were going to be handed on to his grandson. So the poet's personal link with the future – the repository of all his creative life – was this young boy who, in this poem, is reading aloud to him on his bed beside the unpainted screen. It sums up much that I feel is inherent in the two-way grandparent-grandchild relationship: the trust, the sense of psychological safety that each party can derive from the other, the changing, reversible roles. The fact that it was written over a thousand years ago is irrelevant. It speaks to us of an age-old relationship, one that both evolves out of linear time and transcends it.

Richard Bentley

Richard Cumberland's memoirs give a picture of his grand-father somewhat at odds with his contemporary reputation. Dr Bentley (1662–1742) was a classicist and Fellow of the Royal Society; he was also Master of Trinity College, Cambridge, where for 30 years he fought a running battle with the fellows over his autocratic handling of college affairs. They tried to get rid of him several times, enlisting the help of the Bishop of Ely (mentioned in this extract), but the learned doctor refused to be dislodged.

Of Doctor Richard Bentley, my maternal grandfather, I shall next take leave to speak. Of him I have perfect recollection. His person, his dignity, his language and his love fixed my early attention, and stamped both his image and his words upon my memory. . . .

I had a sister somewhat elder than myself. Had there been any of that sternness in my grandfather, which is so falsely imputed to him, it may well be supposed we should have been awed into silence in his presence, to which we were admitted every day. Nothing can be further from the truth; he was the unwearied patron and promoter of all our childish sports and sallies; at all times ready to detach himself from any topic of conversation to take an interest and bear his part in our amusements. The eager curiosity natural to our age, and the questions it gave birth to, so teazing to many parents, he, on the contrary, attended to and encouraged, as the claims of infant reason never to be evaded or abused; strongly recommending, that to all such enquiries answer should be given according to the strictest truth, and information dealt to us in the clearest terms, as a sacred duty never to be departed from. I have broken in upon him many a time in his hours of study, when he would put his book aside, ring his hand-bell for his servant, and be led to his shelves to take down a picture-book for my amusement. I do not say that his good-nature always gained its object, as the pictures which his books generally supplied me with were anatomical drawings of dissected bodies, very little calculated to communicate delight; but he had nothing better to produce. . . .

Once, and only once, I recollect his giving me a gentle rebuke for making a most outrageous noise in the room over his library and disturbing him in his studies; I had no apprehension of anger from him; and confidently answered that I could not help it, as I had been at battledore and shuttle cock with Master Gooch, the Bishop of Ely's son. 'And I have been at this sport with his father,' he replied; 'but thine has been the more amusing game; so there's no harm done.'

He recommended it as a very essential duty in parents to be particularly attentive to the first dawnings of reason in their children; and his own practice was the best illustration of his doctrine; for he was the most patient hearer and most favourable interpreter of first attempts at argument and meaning that I ever knew. When I was rallied by my mother, for roundly asserting that *I never slept*, I remember full well his calling on me to account for it; and when I explained it by saying I never knew myself to be asleep, and therefore supposed I never slept at all, he gave me credit for my defence, and said to my mother, 'Leave your boy in possession of his opinion; he has as clear a conception of sleep, and at least as comfortable an one, as the philosophers who puzzle their brains about it, and do not rest so well.'

ALFRED LORD TENNYSON (1809–1892)

To Alfred Tennyson – My Grandson

In the original manuscript this poem was dedicated: 'To Alfred Tennyson, babe, from Alfred Tennyson, septuagenarian.'

Golden-hair'd Ally whose name is one with mine
Crazy with laughter and babble and earth's new wine,
Now that the flower of a year and a half is thine,
O little blossom, O mine, and mine of mine,
Glorious poet who never hast written a line,
Laugh, for the name at the head of my verse is thine.
May'st thou never be wrong'd by the name that is mine!

MAXIM GORKY (1869–1936)

from

My Childhood

After the death of his father from cholera, Maxim Gorky and his mother went to live with her parents. In this passage Maxim, aged five, is going with his mother and grandmother by Volga steamer to Nizhny Novgorod where his grandparents lived.

The ship's voice, overhead, quieted down; the vibrations of the boat and its movements in the water stopped. Dripping walls opposite the porthole shut off the air and the light, and the cabin grew stifling and dark. The bundles among which I had been placed seemed to grow larger and harder, and I began to feel crushed by them. A fear that I had been left all alone and for good in that empty ship possessed me.

I tried the door, but the metal handle was unbudging. I picked up a bottle of milk and put all my strength in the blow I gave it to make it turn; but all I accomplished was to break the bottle and spill the milk, which splashed over me and trickled down my legs. Sobbing with exasperation, I cried myself to sleep on the bundles.

I woke to find the boat in motion and the porthole round and glowing like a sun. Beside me sat grandma, combing her hair back from her knitted brows and muttering to herself. Her blue-black hair was remarkable for its abundance. It came below her knees and even reached the ground. She had to hold it up with one hand while, with the other, she drew an almost toothless comb through the heavy mass. The strain made her lips purse and brought an exasperated sharpness to her eyes. There was something almost bitter in her expression; yet, when I asked why her hair was so long, it was in her usual melodious words and with her customary tender intonations that she answered, 'God must have given it to me to punish me. It's combed out but look at it! When I was a girl I was proud of that mane but now I curse it. But sleep, child. It's early yet. The sun's barely up.'

'I want to get up.'

'Well then, get up,' she said. As she braided her hair she glanced toward my mother who lay rigid on her bunk. 'How did you happen to break that bottle? Tell me, but be quiet about it.' That was her way. Her words were like music and like flowers. They bloom in my memory like everlasting blossoms. I remember her smile as a dilation of her large eyes and a cheerful flash of her white teeth that gave her face an inexpressible charm. Despite her wrinkles and her weathered complexion she looked young and even glowing. All that spoiled her appearance was her bulbous, red nose with its splayed-out nostrils, the result of a weakness for drink and her snuff-taking; her black snuff box was almost always in her hand. Outwardly she looked dark, but within burned a vigorous, inextinguishable flame of which the radiance in her eyes was a reflection. She was so stooped as to be almost hunchbacked, yet her motions were gliding and light like those of a great cat; and she was soft and caressing like a cat.

I felt that I had been asleep and in darkness until she came, and that then I woke and was led into the light. It was she who provided the threads with which my mind wove its multi-colored patterns. And by this she became my lifelong friend, the dearest and most understanding and the closest to my heart. Nourished by her wise love for every living thing, I gained the strength to face a hard life.

MARCEL PROUST (1871–1922)

from

Remembrance of Things Past

In this fictionalised account of a stay with his grandmother, Proust is a boy of about 12. Because of his poor health (he suffered from asthma) his parents decided he should spend his holidays in Normandy, with her. In later life he referred to 'those seaside holidays when grandmother and I, lost in one another, walked battling with the wind and talking'. On this occasion the scene is evening. The boy, weakened by fever, is waiting for his grandmother to help him to bed.

She was wearing a loose cambric dressing-gown which she put on at home whenever any of us was ill (because she felt more comfortable in it, she used to say, for she always ascribed selfish motives to her actions), and which was, for tending us, for watching by our beds, her servant's smock, her nurse's uniform, her nun's habit. But whereas the attentions of servants, nurses and nuns, their kindness to us, the merits we find in them and the gratitude we owe them, increase the impression we have of being, in their eyes, someone else, of feeling that we are alone, keeping in our own hands the control over our thoughts, our will to live, I knew, when I was with my grandmother, that however great the misery that there was in me, it would be received by her with a pity still more vast, that everything that was mine, my cares, my wishes, would be buttressed, in my grandmother, by a desire to preserve and enhance my life that was altogether stronger than was my own; and my thoughts were continued and extended in her without undergoing the slightest deflection, since they passed from my mind into hers without any change of atmosphere or of personality. And – like a man who tries to fasten his tie in front of a glass and forgets that the end which he sees reflected is not on the side to which he raises his hand, or like a dog that chases along the ground the dancing shadow of an insect in the air – misled by her appearance in the body as we are apt to be in this world where we have no direct perception of people's souls, I threw myself into the arms of my grandmother and pressed my lips to her face as though I were thus gaining access to that immense heart which she opened to me. And when I felt my mouth glued to her cheeks, to her brow, I drew from them something so beneficial, so nourishing, that I remained as motionless, as solemn, as calmly gluttonous as a babe at the breast.

Afterwards I gazed inexhaustibly at her large face, outlined like a beautiful cloud, glowing and serene, behind which I could discern the radiance of her tender love. And everything that received, in however slight a degree, any share of her sensations, everything that could be said to belong in any way to her was at once so spiritualised, so sanctified that with outstretched hands I smoothed her beautiful hair, still hardly grey, with as much respect, precaution and gentleness as if I had actually been caressing her goodness. She found such pleasure in taking any trouble that saved me one, and in a moment of immobility and rest for my weary limbs something so exquisite, that when, having seen that she wished to help me undress and go to bed, I made as though to stop her and to undress myself, with an imploring gaze she arrested my hands as they fumbled with the top buttons of my jacket and my boots.

'Oh, do let me!' she begged. 'It's such a joy for your Granny. And be sure you knock on the wall if you want anything in the night. My bed is just on the other side, and the partition is quite thin. Just give a knock now, as soon as you're in bed, so that we shall know where we are.'

And, sure enough, that evening I gave three knocks – a signal which, a week later, when I was ill, I repeated every morning for several days, because my grandmother wanted me to have some milk early. Then, when I thought that I could hear her stirring – so that she should not be kept waiting but might, the moment she had brought me the milk, go to sleep again – I would venture three little taps, timidly, faintly, but for all that distinctly, for if I was afraid of disturbing her in case I had been mistaken and she was still asleep, neither did I wish her to lie awake listening for a summons which she had not at once caught and which I should not have the heart to repeat. And scarcely had I given my taps than I heard three others, in a different tone from mine, stamped with a calm authority, repeated twice over so that there should be no mistake, and saying to me plainly: 'Don't get agitated; I've heard you; I shall be with you in a minute!' and shortly afterwards my grandmother would appear. I would explain to her that I had been afraid she would not hear me, or might think that it was someone in the room beyond who was tapping; at which she would smile: 'Mistake my poor pet's knocking for anyone else's! Why, Granny could tell it a mile away! Do you suppose there's anyone else in the world who's such a silly-billy, with such febrile little knuckles, so afraid of waking me up and of not making me understand? Even if it just gave the tiniest scratch, Granny could tell her mouse's sound at once, especially such a poor miserable little mouse as mine is. I could hear it just now, trying to make up its mind, and rustling the bedclothes, and going through all its tricks.'

She would push open the shutters, and where a wing of the hotel jutted out at right angles to my window, the sun would already have settled on the roof, like a slater who is up betimes, and starts early and works quietly so as not to rouse the sleeping town whose stillness makes him seem more agile. She would tell me what time it was, what sort of day it would be, that it was not worth while my getting up and coming to the window, that there was a mist over the sea, whether the baker's shop had opened yet, what the vehicle was that I could hear passing – that whole trifling curtain-raiser, that insignificant introit of a new day which no one attends, a little scrap of life which was only for our two selves, but which I should have no hesitation in evoking, later on, to Françoise or even to strangers, speaking of the fog 'which you could have cut with a knife' at six o'clock that morning, with the ostentation of one who was boasting not of a piece of knowledge that he had acquired but of a mark of affection shown to himself alone; sweet morning moment which opened like a symphony with the rhythmical dialogue of my three taps, to which the thin wall of my bedroom, steeped in love and joy, grown melodious, incorporeal, singing like the angelic choir, responded with three other taps, eagerly awaited, repeated once again, in which it contrived to waft to me the soul of my grandmother, whole and perfect, and the promise of her coming, with the swiftness of an annunciation and a musical fidelity.

from

Childhood, Boyhood, Youth

Tolstoy's mother died when he was barely two, and in this account of his grandmother's name-day he describes his anguish as a ten-year-old at the thought of saying anything that might belittle her memory. 'Maman', he said later, 'is my highest image of love.' However, when he himself became a father he had different ideas: 'I don't care for children till they are 2 or 3 years old . . . There are two types of men: hunters and non hunters. Non hunters love babies . . . Hunters are terrified . . . I know of no exception to this rule.' But he must have inspired affection in his grandchildren: one of them, witnessing a turbulent scene between Tolstoy and his wife, burst into tears on leaving them, weeping for 'grandmother and grandfather'.

Nearly a month after we moved to Moscow I was sitting upstairs in my grandmother's house at a large table, writing. Opposite me sat our drawing-master, putting some finishing touches to the head of a Turk in a turban, executed in black crayon. Volodya, craning his neck, was standing behind the drawing-master and looking over his shoulder. This head was Volodya's first effort in crayon and was to be presented to grandmamma that very day, her name-day.

'What about some more shadow here?' said Volodya, rising on tiptoe and pointing to the Turk's neck.

'No, it is not necessary,' said the master, putting away the crayon and holder into a box with a sliding lid. 'It is all right now: don't touch it any more. Well, Nikolai [Tolstoy's second name],' he added, standing up and continuing to examine the Turk out of the corner of his eye, 'won't you tell us your great secret at last – what are you going to give your grandmother? I really think it would have been better if you too had drawn a head. Well, good-bye young gentlemen,' he said, taking his hat and his ticket* and departing.

At that moment I was thinking myself that a head would have been better than what I was working at. When we had been told that it would soon be our grandmother's name-day and that we ought to prepare presents to give her the idea occurred to me of writing some verses for the occasion, and I immediately made up two verses with rhymes, hoping to do the rest just as easily. I really do not know how the idea – such a peculiar one for a child – entered my head but I do remember that I was very pleased with it and that to all questions on the subject I replied that I would certainly have a present for grandmamma but was not going to say what it was.

Contrary to my expectations I found that after composing two verses in the first heat of enthusiasm, try as I would I could not produce any more. I began to read the different poems in our books; but neither Dmitriev nor Derzhavin helped me at all – far from it, they convinced me still more of my own inability. Knowing that Karl Ivanych [the German tutor] was fond of transcribing verses, I began surreptitiously burrowing among his papers, and among some German poems I found one in Russian which he must have written himself.

* A master was given a ticket at the end of each lesson, which he saved and later presented for payment.

To Madame L – Petrovsk, 3 June 1825

Remember me near,
Remember me far,
O remember me
Henceforth and for ever.
Remember to my grave
How truly I can love.

This poem, penned in a beautiful round hand on a sheet of fine letterpaper, attracted me by the touching feeling with which it was imbued. I immediately learned it by heart and decided to take it as a model. The matter then went much more easily. By the name-day twelve lines of good wishes were ready, and sitting at the schoolroom table I was copying them out on vellum.

Two sheets were already spoilt . . . not because I had found it necessary to make any alterations (my verses seemed to me perfect) but because after the third line the tail-end of each successive one would go curving up and up so that even from a distance they looked crooked and no good at all.

The third sheet came out as sloping as the others but I decided not to do it again. In my poem I wished grandmamma many happy returns of the day, and concluded thus:

To comfort thee we shall endeavour,
And love thee like our own dear mother.

This ought to have sounded really quite fine yet in a strange way the last line offended my ear.

'And to lo-ve thee li-ike our own dear mo-ther,' I kept repeating to myself. 'What other rhyme could I use instead of *mother*? . . . Oh, it will do! It's better than Karl Ivanych's anyhow.'

Accordingly I added the last line to the rest. Then in our bedroom I read the whole composition aloud with expression and gestures. There were some lines that did not scan at all but I did not dwell on them: the last line, however, struck me even more forcibly and disagreeably than before. I sat on my bed and pondered:

'Why did I write *like our own dear mother?* She is not here so there was no need ever to bring her in; it is true, I do love and respect grandmamma, still she is not the same as . . . Why did I put that? Why did I write a lie? Of course it's only poetry but I needn't have done *that.*'

At this point the tailor entered with our new suits. 'Well, it can't be helped!' I thought irritably, stuffing my verses under the pillow in my vexation, and ran to try on my Moscow clothes.

They were splendid: the cinnamon-brown jackets with their bronze buttons fitted tightly – not as they made them in the country to allow for growing. The black trousers, also close-fitting, showed up our muscles and came down over our boots.

'At last I've got real trousers with straps!' I reflected, beside myself with delight as I examined my legs from every side. Although the new garments felt very tight and uncomfortable I concealed the fact from everybody and declared that, on the contrary, they fitted comfortably and if there was any fault about them it was that they were, if anything, a shade loose. After that I stood for a long time before the looking-glass, brushing my generously pomaded hair; but strive as I would I could not smooth down the tufts of hair on the crown of my head: so soon as, to test their obedience, I stopped pressing them with the brush they rose and stuck out in all directions, imparting to my face a most ridiculous look.

Karl Ivanych was dressing in another room, and his

blue frock-coat and some white things were carried in to him through the schoolroom. The voice of one of grandmamma's maids was heard at the door which led downstairs and I went out to see what she wanted. She was holding in her hand a stiffly starched shirt-front which she told me she had brought for Karl Ivanych, and that she had been up all night to get it washed in time. I undertook to deliver the shirt-front and asked whether grandmamma was up yet.

'I should say so! She's had her coffee and now the priest is here. What a fine fellow you look!' she added with a smile, surveying my new clothes.

This remark made me blush. I whirled round on one leg, snapped my fingers and gave a little skip, to let her feel that she still did not thoroughly appreciate what a very fine fellow I was.

When I took Karl Ivanych his shirt-front he no longer needed it: he had put on another and, stooping before a small looking-glass that stood on a table, was holding the magnificent knot of his cravat in both hands and trying whether his smoothly shaved chin could move easily in and out. After pulling our clothes straight all round and asking Nikolai to do the same for him he took us down to grandmamma. I laugh when I remember how strongly all three of us smelt of pomatum as we descended the stairs.

Karl Ivanych was carrying a little box he had made himself, Volodya had his drawing and I my verses; and each of us had on the tip of his tongue the greeting with which he intended to offer his present. When Karl Ivanych opened the drawing-room door the priest was putting on his vestments and we heard the first sounds of the *Te Deum*.

Grandmamma was already in the drawing-room: with her head bowed and resting her hands on the back of a chair she was standing by the wall, praying devoutly; papa stood beside her. He turned towards us and smiled as he saw us hastily hide our presents behind our backs and stop just inside the door in an effort to escape notice. The whole effect of a surprise, on which we had counted, was lost.

When the time came to go up and kiss the cross I suddenly felt myself suffering from an insurmountable paralysing fit of shyness, and feeling that I should never have the courage to give my present I hid behind the back of Karl Ivanych who, having expressed his good wishes in the choicest of phrases, transferred his little box from his right hand to his left, presented it to grandmamma and stepped a few paces to one side to make way for Volodya. Grandmamma seemed delighted with the box, which had gilt strips pasted round the borders, and expressed her gratitude with the sweetest of smiles. It was evident, however, that she did not know where to put the box, and probably for this reason she asked papa to look at it and see how wonderfully skilfully it was made.

After satisfying his curiosity papa handed it to the priest, who apparently admired the little article very much indeed: he nodded his head, gazing with interest first at the box, then at the craftsman who could make such a beautiful object. Volodya presented his Turk, and he too received the most flattering praise from all sides. I was the next and grandmamma turned towards me with an encouraging smile.

Those who have experienced what it is to be shy know that the sensation increases in direct proportion to its duration, and that one's resolution diminishes in the same ratio: in other words, the longer the condition lasts the more invincible it becomes and the less resolution remains.

The last remnants of courage and resolution forsook me while Karl Ivanych and Volodya were offering their presents, and my shyness reached its climax: I felt the blood continually rushing from my heart to my head, my face kept changing colour and great drops of perspiration stood out on my forehead and my nose. My ears were burning, I felt my whole body trembling and cold with perspiration, and I shifted from one foot to the other but did not budge from the spot.

'Well, Nikolai, show us what you have got – is it a box or a drawing?' papa said to me. There was no help for it: with a shaking hand I held out the crumpled fatal roll; but my voice utterly refused to serve me and I stood before grandmamma in silence. I could not get away from the dreadful idea that instead of the expected drawing my good-for-nothing verses would be read out in front of everybody, and the words *like our own dear mother* would clearly prove that I had never loved her and had forgotten her.

How can I describe my sufferings when grandmamma began to read my poem aloud, and when, unable to make it out, she paused in the middle of a line to glance at papa with what seemed to me then a mocking smile, or when she failed to give a word the expression I had intended, and when, on account of her weak eyesight, she handed the sheet to papa before she had finished, and asked him to read it all over again from the beginning. I thought she did so because she had had enough of reading such stupid crookedly-written verses, and so that papa might read for himself that last line which was such plain proof of want of feeling. I expected him to give me a rap on the nose with the verses and say, 'You horrid boy, you are not to forget your mother . . . take that!' But nothing of the kind happened: on the contrary, when it had been read to the end grandmamma said *'Charmant!'* and kissed me on the forehead.

The little box, the drawing and the poem were laid out in a row beside two cambric handkerchiefs and a snuff-box with a portrait of mamma on the lid on the adjustable flap of the arm-chair in which grandmamma always sat.

'The Princess Varvara Ilinichna!' announced one of the two huge footmen who stood behind grandmamma's carriage when she drove out.

But grandmamma was gazing thoughtfully at the portrait set in the tortoise-shell snuff-box, and made no reply.

'Shall I show her in, your ladyship?' repeated the footman.

DAVID MALOUF (1934–)

At My Grandmother's

David Malouf's poem harks back to his childhood in Australia. The tension between continuity and change, a recurring theme in his poetry, underlies his imagery here. An oppressive sense of the interweaving of present and past weighs on the mind of the young boy as he holds the skeins of wool for his grandmother.

An afternoon, late summer, in a room
Shuttered against the bright, envenomed leaves;
An under-water world, where time, like water,
Was held in the wide arms of a gilded clock,
And my grandmother, turning in the still sargasso
Of memory, wound out her griefs and held
A small boy prisoner to weeds and corals,
While summer leaked its daylight through his head.

I feared that room, the parrot screeching soundless
In its dome of glass, the faded butterflies
Like jewels pinned against a sable cloak,
And my grandmother winding out the skeins I held
Like trickling time, between my outstretched arms;

Feared most of all the stiff, bejewelled fingers
Pinned at her throat, or moving on grey wings
From word to word; and feared her voice that called
Down from their gilded frames the ghosts of children
Who played at hoop and ball, whose spindrift faces
(The drowned might wear such smiles) looked out across
The wreck and debris of the years, to where
A small boy sat, as they once sat, and held
In the wide ache of his arms, all time, like water,
And watched the old grey hands wind out his blood.

from

Childhood: With Grandmother

*Isaac Babel was the son of a Jewish tradesman in Odessa.
He wrote his stories in Russian, but with his grandmother he
would have spoken Yiddish, the language of the Jews of
Eastern Europe.*

This Sabbath afternoon was supposed to be spent with
Grandmother. She had a separate room right at the back of
the flat, behind the kitchen. In a corner of the room stood a
stove: Grandmother always suffered from cold. The room
was hot and stuffy, and this always made me depressed and
feel I wanted to escape to freedom.

Through to Grandmother's room I dragged my stuff,
my books, my music stand and my violin. The table was
already set for me. Grandmother sat down in the corner.
I ate. We said nothing. The door was closed. We were alone.
For dinner there was gefilte fish with horseradish sauce (for
which it is worth becoming a Jew), a rich, tasty soup, roast
meat with onions, salad, compote, coffee, pie and apples.
I ate it all. I was a dreamer, that was true, but a dreamer with
a big appetite. Grandmother cleared away the crockery. The
room was now tidy. In the window stood wilted flowers. Of
all living creation, Grandmother loved her son, her grandson, the dog Mimka and flowers. And Mimka arrived too,
curled up on the sofa and fell asleep at once. She was a

terrible sleepy-head, but a wonderful dog, good-hearted, sensible, small and pretty. Mimka was a pug-dog. Her coat was light in colour. Even in old age she never grew fat or flabby, never put on weight, but remained shapely and slender. She lived with us a long time, from birth to death, the whole of her fifteen years' doggy life, and loved us – quite plainly, and most of all Grandmother, who was stern and without mercy to anyone. What friends they were, silent and secretive, I shall tell another time. It is a very good, touching and tender story.

And so, we were three – Grandmother, Mimi and I. Mimi slept. Grandmother, in a good mood, wearing her best silk dress, sat in the corner, and I was supposed to do my homework. That day was a hard one for me. I had had six lessons at the grammar school, and Mr Sorokin, my music teacher, was supposed to be coming, as was Mr L., the Hebrew teacher, to give me a lesson I had missed, and then perhaps also Monsieur Peysson, the French teacher, and the lessons had to be prepared. With L. I could cope, we were old friends, but the music and the scales – what misery! First I got down to my homework. I laid out my exercise books, began carefully to work out the problems. Grandmother did not interrupt me, God forbid. Her tension, her reverence for my work gave her face a stupid look. Her eyes, round, yellow, transparent, never left me. Whenever I turned a page they would slowly follow my hand. Anyone else would have found her persistently observing, ceaseless gaze very hard to put up with, but I was used to it.

Then Grandmother heard my lessons. Russian, it should be said, she spoke badly, distorting the words in her own peculiar way, mixing Russian ones with Polish and Hebrew. She could not read or write Russian, of course, and held the book upside down. But this did not prevent me from reciting the lesson to her from beginning to end. Grandmother listened, understood none of it, but the music of the words was sweet to her, she went in awe of learning, believed me, believed in me and wanted me to become a *bogatyr* (a hero in Russian folklore) – such was her name for a man who was rich (*bogaty*). I finished the lessons and proceeded to read a book – I was reading Turgenev's *First Love* at the time. I liked everything in it, the clear words, the descriptions, the conversations, but trembled at the scene where Vladimir's father strikes Zinaida on the cheek with his horsewhip. I heard the whistle of the whip, the supple leather dug into me keenly, painfully, instantaneously. I was seized by an inexplicable excitement. At that point I had to stop reading, walk about the room. Meanwhile, Grandmother sat immovable, and even the hot, heavy air did not stir, as though it knew I was studying and must not be disturbed. The heat in the room kept increasing. Mimka began to snore. And earlier it had been quiet, ghostly quiet, not a sound had been heard. At that moment it all seemed extraordinary to me and made me want to flee from it and yet remain for ever. The darkening room, Grandmother's yellow eyes, her small figure, wrapped in a shawl, doubled up and silent in the corner, the hot air, the closed door, and the smack of the whip and that penetrating whistle – only now do I understand how strange it was, how much it meant to me. From this troubled state I was delivered by the doorbell. Sorokin had arrived. At that moment I hated him, hated the scales, that incomprehensible, superfluous, shrill music. It must be admitted that this Sorokin was a good fellow, wore his black hair in a crew cut, had large red hands and full red lips. That day under Grandmother's eye he was to work for a whole hour, even more, was to exert himself to the utmost. All this got not the slightest recognition. Grandmother's eyes followed his movements coldly and tenaciously, remaining indifferent and alien to him. Grandmother took no interest in people from outside. She required that they fulfil their obligations to us, and that was all. We began the lesson. It was not that I was afraid of

Grandmother, but for a solid hour I had to experience upon my person the immoderate zeal of poor Sorokin. He felt very out of place in this remote room, in front of a peacefully sleeping dog and a hostile, coldly watching old woman. At last he began to take his leave. Grandmother indifferently gave him her large, firm wrinkled hand without even moving it. As he went out, he caught hold of a chair.

I endured the following hour as well – Mr L.'s lesson, and awaited the moment when the door would close behind him, too.

Evening came. Distant, golden points caught fire in the heavens. Our courtyard – a deep cage – was blinded by the moon. In the neighbours' house a female voice had begun to sing the romance 'Why Do I Madly Love?'. My family had gone to the theatre. I grew sad. I was tired. I had read so much, studied so much, seen so much. Grandmother lit a lamp. Her room at once became quiet: the dark, heavy furniture was gently illumined. Mimi woke up, padded about the rooms, came back again and began to wait for supper. The maid brought the samovar. Grandmother was very fond of tea. For me, there was gingerbread. We drank in great quantity. In Grandmother's deep, sharp wrinkles sweat began to gleam. 'Are you sleepy?' she asked. 'No,' I answered. We began to talk. And again I heard Grandmother's stories. Long ago, many years past, a certain Jew had run an inn. He was poor, married, burdened with children and traded in illicit vodka. The police commissioner came and harassed him. He began to find life difficult. He went to see the *tsadik* [Hassidic rabbi] and said, 'Rebbe, the police commissioner is vexing me to death. Intercede for me with God.' 'Go in peace,' the *tsadik* said to him. 'The police commissioner will settle down.' The Jew went away. In the doorway of his inn he found the police commissioner. The latter lay dead with a purple, swollen face.

Grandmother fell silent. The samovar hissed. The woman next door went on singing. The moon went on dazzling. Mimi wagged her tail. She was hungry.

'In the old days people had faith,' said Grandmother. 'Life was simpler then. When I was a girl the Poles rose up in rebellion. Near us there was a Polish count's manor. The tsar himself came to see the count. For seven days and nights there was carousing there. At night I ran to the count's castle and looked in through the lighted windows. The count had a daughter and the finest pearls in the world. Then there was the uprising. Soldiers came and dragged him out to the square. We all stood around and wept. The soldiers dug a pit. They wanted to blindfold the old man. He said "I don't need one," stood facing the soldiers and ordered, "Fire!" The count was a tall, grey-haired man. The muzhiks [Russian peasants] loved him.

'As they were beginning to bury him, a messenger arrived in haste. He had brought a reprieve from the tsar.'

The samovar had gone out. Grandmother poured a final, cold glass of tea, and sucked a piece of sugar in her toothless mouth.'

'Your grandfather,' she began, 'knew a lot of stories, but he didn't have faith in anything, all he had faith in was human beings. He lent all his money to friends, and when he went to see them they threw him downstairs, and his mind became touched.' And Grandmother told me about my grandfather, a tall, sarcastic, passionate and despotic man. He played the violin, wrote at nights and knew all the languages. He was possessed by an unquenchable thirst for knowledge and life. A general's daughter fell in love with their eldest son, he saw a great deal of the world, played cards and died in Canada at the age of thirty-seven. Grandmother had only one son left, and me. It was all over. Day inclines towards evening, and death approaches slowly. Grandmother falls silent, inclines her head and weeps. 'Study,' she says with force, 'study, you will attain everything – wealth and fame. You must know everything. Everyone will fall down and abase themselves before you. Everyone must envy you. Don't have faith in human beings. Don't have friends. Don't lend them money. Don't lend them your heart.'

Grandmother does not say any more. Silence. Grandmother thinks of the years and sorrows that are past, thinks about my fate, and her stern precept is heavily – for ever – laid upon my weak child's shoulders. In the dark corner the incandescent cast-iron stove gives out an intense heat. I cannot breathe, there is nothing to breathe, I must run outside to fresh air, to freedom, but I have no strength to raise my drooping head.

In the kitchen there is a clatter of crockery. Grandmother goes there. We are getting ready to have supper. Soon I hear her metallic, angry voice. She is shouting at the maid. I feel strange and hurt. After all just now she was breathing peace and sadness. The maid snarls back. 'Get out of here, hireling,' the intolerably high voice rings out with uncontainable fury. 'I am the mistress here. You are destroying our property. Out.' I cannot endure this deafening, iron shout. Through the half-open door I can see Grandmother, her face strained, her lower lip quivering finely and mercilessly, her throat distended as though it were swollen. The maid makes some retort. 'Go,' said Grandmother. It has grown quiet. The maid has bowed and, inaudibly, as though afraid of offending the silence, crept out of the room.

We eat our supper in silence. We eat well, abundantly and at length. Grandmother's transparent eyes are immobile and where they are looking, I do not know. After supper she . . .

More than that I do not see, for I sleep very soundly, sleep a youthful sleep behind seven seals in Grandmother's hot room.

LADY MARY WORTLEY MONTAGU
(1689–1762)

A letter to her daughter, the Countess of Bute

Lady Mary Wortley Montagu was famous for her letters, which were published after her death. She travelled widely with her husband, who was a Member of Parliament and diplomat, and was part of the literary scene around the court of George I (where her husband's knowledge of foreign languages came in useful with a king who could speak no English). She was someone of great energy, an avid reader, and frequently had advice on the subject of children's education for her daughter (with one surprising caveat – that she hoped her granddaughter would not marry).

Lovere
January 10, 1752

My Dear Child,

I am extremely concerned to hear you complain of ill health, at a time of life when you ought to be in the flower of your strength. I hope I need not recommend to you the care of it: the tenderness you have for your children is sufficient to enforce you to the utmost regard for the preservation of a life so necessary to their well being. I do not doubt your prudence in their education: neither can I say any thing particular relating to it at this distance, different tempers requiring different management. In general, never attempt to govern them (as most people do) by deceit: if they find themselves cheated, even in trifles, it will so far lessen the authority of their instructor, as to make them neglect all their future admonitions. And, if possible, breed them free from prejudices; those contracted in the nursery often influence the whole life after, of which I have seen many melancholy examples. . . . If your daughters are inclined to love reading, do not check their inclination by hindering them of the diverting part of it; it is as necessary for the amusement of women as the reputation of men; but teach them not to expect or desire any applause from it. Let their brothers shine, and let them content themselves with making their lives easier by it, which I experimentally know is more effectually done by study than any other way. Ignorance is as much the fountain of vice as idleness, and indeed generally produces it. People that do not read, or work for a livelihood, have many hours they know not how to employ; especially women, who commonly fall into vapours, or something worse. I am afraid you'll think this letter very tedious: forgive it as coming from your most affectionate mother.

MW

BERTRAND RUSSELL (1872–1970)

from

The Autobiography of Bertrand Russell

Bertrand Russell's parents died when he was a child and he went to live in his grandparents' house in Pembroke Lodge, Richmond Park. His grandfather Lord John Russell, who had pioneered the first Reform Bill through Parliament in 1832 and later became Prime Minister, died when he was a boy. His grandmother remained a central influence on his early life. He himself, one of the most remarkable men of this century, became a philosopher, writer and Nobel Prize winner; he remained politically active in the cause of peace and nuclear disarmament into his nineties (when he was briefly imprisoned for civil disobedience).

My grandfather as I remember him was a man well past eighty, being wheeled round the garden in a bath chair, or sitting in his room reading Hansard. I was just six years old when he died. I remember that when on the day of his death I saw my brother (who was at school) drive up in a cab although it was in the middle of term, I shouted 'Hurrah!', and my nurse said: 'Hush! You must not say "Hurrah" today!' It may be inferred from this incident that my grandfather had no great importance to me.

My grandmother, on the contrary, who was twenty-three years younger than he was, was the most important person to me throughout my childhood. She was a Scotch

Presbyterian, Liberal in politics and religion (she became a Unitarian at the age of seventy), but extremely strict in all matters of morality. When she married my grandfather she was young and very shy. My grandfather was a widower with two children and four step-children, and a few years after their marriage he became Prime Minister. For her this must have been a severe ordeal. She related how she went once as a girl to one of the famous breakfasts given by the poet Rogers, and how, after observing her shyness, he said: 'Have a little tongue. You need it my dear!' It was obvious from her conversation that she never came anywhere near to knowing what it feels like to be in love. She told me once how relieved she was on her honeymoon when her mother joined her. On another occasion she lamented that so much poetry should be concerned with so trivial a subject as love. But she made my grandfather a devoted wife, and never, so far as I have been able to discover, failed to perform what her very exacting standards represented as her duty.

As a mother and a grandmother she was deeply, but not always wisely, solicitous. I do not think that she ever understood the claims of animal spirits and exuberant vitality. She demanded that everything should be viewed through a mist of Victorian sentiment. I remember trying to make her see that it was inconsistent to demand at one and the same time that everybody should be well housed, and yet that no new houses should be built because they were an eye-sore. To her each sentiment had its separate rights, and must not be asked to give place to another sentiment on account of anything so cold as mere logic. She was cultivated according to the standards of her time; she could speak French, German and Italian faultlessly, without the slightest trace of accent. She knew Shakespeare, Milton, and the eighteenth-century poets intimately. She could repeat the signs of the Zodiac and the names of the Nine Muses. She had a minute knowledge of English history according to the Whig tradition. French, German, and Italian classics were familiar to her. Of politics since 1880 she had a close personal knowledge. But everything that involved reasoning had been totally omitted from her education, and was absent from her mental life. She never could understand how locks on rivers worked, although I heard any number of people try to explain it to her. Her morality was that of a Victorian Puritan, and nothing would have persuaded her that a man who swore on occasion might nevertheless have some good qualities. . . .

Of psychology in the modern sense, she had, of course, no vestige. Certain motives were known to exist: love of country, public spirit, love of one's children, were laudable motives; love of money, love of power, vanity, were bad motives. Good men acted from good motives always; bad men, however, even the worst, had moments when they were not wholly bad. Marriage was a puzzling institution. It was clearly the duty of husbands and wives to love one another, but it was a duty they ought not to perform too easily, for if sex attraction drew them together there must be something not quite nice about them. Not, of course, that she would have phrased the matter in these terms. What she would have said, and in fact did say, was: 'You know, I never think that the affection of husbands and wives is quite such a good thing as the affection of parents for their children, because there is sometimes something a little selfish about it.' That was as near as her thoughts could come to such a topic as sex. Perhaps once I heard her approach a little nearer to the forbidden topic: that was when she said that Lord Palmerston had been peculiar among men through the fact that he was not quite a good man. She disliked wine, abhorred tobacco, and was always on the verge of becoming a vegetarian. Her life was austere. She ate only the plainest food, breakfasted at eight, and until she reached the age of eighty, never sat in a comfortable chair until after tea. She was completely unworldly, and despised those who thought anything of worldly honours. I regret to say that her attitude to Queen Victoria was far from respectful. She used to relate with much amusement how one time when she was at Windsor and feeling rather ill, the Queen had been graciously pleased to say: 'Lady Russell may sit down. Lady So-and-So shall stand in front of her.'

After I reached the age of fourteen, my grandmother's intellectual limitations became trying to me, and her Puritan morality began to seem to me to be excessive; but while I was a child her great affection for me, and her intense care for my welfare, made me love her and gave me that feeling of safety that children need. I remember when I was about four or five years old lying awake thinking how dreadful it would be when my grandmother was dead. When she did in fact die, which was after I was married, I did not mind at all. But in retrospect, as I have grown older, I have realised more and more the importance she had in moulding my outlook on life. Her fearlessness, her public spirit, her contempt for convention, and her indifference to the opinion of the majority have always seemed good to me and have impressed themselves upon me as worthy of imitation. She gave me a Bible with her favourite texts written on the fly-leaf. Among these was 'Thou shalt not follow a multitude to do evil'. Her emphasis upon this text led me in later life to be not afraid of belonging to small minorities.

from

The Old Curiosity Shop

Dickens liked to be called 'Venerables' by his grandchildren, a title he considered less ageing than 'Grandfather'. His eldest grandchild wrote an account of him which is in piquant contrast to the idealised relationship in The Old Curiosity Shop, *the book that won the hearts of his reading public. His granddaughter remembered him as 'Handsome, alert, full of zest . . . laughing and talking at a great rate'; but when he looked down at her, 'I, a very small girl in a pinafore, look up at him. And I am afraid.' If she was playing in the garden while he was writing she felt 'a vague sense of dread, only to be described as "creepy"'. Perhaps this grandchild, like Tolstoy's, found it hard to feel completely at ease in a house dominated by a genius.*

One night I had roamed into the city, and was walking slowly on in my usual way, musing upon a great many things, when I was arrested by an inquiry, the purport of which did not reach me, but which seemed to be addressed to myself, and was preferred in a soft sweet voice that struck me very pleasantly. I turned hastily round, and found at my elbow a pretty little girl, who begged to be directed to a certain street at a considerable distance, and indeed in quite another quarter of the town.

'It is a very long way from here,' said I, 'my child.'

'I know that, sir,' she replied timidly. 'I am afraid it is a very long way; for I came from there, to-night.'

'Alone?' said I, in some surprise.

'Oh yes, I don't mind that, but I am a little frightened now, for I have lost my road.'

'And what made you ask it of me? Suppose I should tell you wrong.'

'I am sure you will not do that,' said the little creature, 'you are such a very old gentleman, and walk so slow yourself.'

I cannot describe how much I was impressed by this appeal, and the energy with which it was made, which brought a tear into the child's clear eye, and made her slight figure tremble as she looked up into my face.

'Come,' said I, 'I'll take you there.'

She put her hand in mine, as confidently as if she had known me from her cradle, and we trudged away together: the little creature accommodating her pace to mine, and rather seeming to lead and take care of me than I to be protecting her. I observed that every now and then she stole a curious look at my face as if to make quite sure that I was not deceiving her, and that these glances (very sharp and keen they were too) seemed to increase her confidence at every repetition.

For my part, my curiosity and interest were, at least, equal to the child's; for child she certainly was, although I thought it probable from what I could make out that her very small and delicate frame imparted a peculiar youthfulness to her appearance. Though more scantily attired than she might have been, she was dressed with perfect neatness, and betrayed no marks of poverty or neglect.

'Who has sent you so far by yourself?' said I.

'Somebody who is very kind to me, sir.'

'And what have you been doing?'

'That, I must not tell,' said the child.

There was something in the manner of this reply which caused me to look at the little creature with an involuntary expression of surprise; for I wondered what kind of errand it might be that occasioned her to be prepared for questioning. Her quick eye seemed to read my thoughts. As it met mine, she added that there was no harm in what she had been doing, but it was a great secret – a secret which she did not even know, herself.

This was said with no appearance of cunning or deceit, but with an unsuspicious frankness that bore the impress of truth. She walked on, as before: growing more familiar with me as we proceeded, and talking cheerfully by the way, but she said no more about her home, beyond remarking that we were going quite a new road and asking if it were a short one.

While we were thus engaged, I revolved in my mind a hundred explanations of the riddle, and rejected them every one. I really felt ashamed to take advantage of the ingenuousness or grateful feeling of the child, for the purpose of gratifying my curiosity. I love these little people; and it is not a slight thing when they, who are so fresh from God, love us. As I had felt pleased, at first, by her confidence, I determined to deserve it, and to do credit to the nature which had prompted her to repose it in me.

There was no reason, however, why I should refrain from seeing the person who had inconsiderately sent her to so great a distance by night and alone; and, as it was not improbable that if she found herself near home she might take farewell of me and deprive me of the opportunity, I avoided the most frequented ways and took the most intricate. Thus it was not until we arrived in the street itself that she knew where we were. Clapping her hands with pleasure, and running on before me for a short distance, my little acquaintance stopped at a door, and remaining on the step till I came up, knocked at it when I joined her.

A part of this door was of glass, unprotected by any shutter; which I did not observe, at first, for all was very dark and silent within, and I was anxious (as indeed the child was also) for an answer to her summons. When she had knocked twice or thrice, there was a noise as if some person were moving inside, and at length a faint light appeared through the glass which, as it approached very slowly – the bearer having to make his way through a great many scattered articles – enabled me to see, both what kind of person it was who advanced, and what kind of place it was through which he came.

He was a little old man with long grey hair, whose face and figure, as he held the light above his head and looked before him as he approached, I could plainly see. Though much altered by age, I fancied I could recognise in his spare and slender form something of that delicate mould which I had noticed in the child. Their bright blue eyes were certainly alike, but his face was so deeply furrowed, and so very full of care, that here all resemblance ceased.

The place through which he made his way at leisure, was one of those receptacles for old and curious things which seem to crouch in odd corners of this town, and to hide their musty treasures from the public eye in jealousy and distrust. There were suits of mail standing like ghosts in armour, here and there; fantastic carvings brought from monkish cloisters; rusty weapons of various kinds; distorted figures in china, and wood, and iron, and ivory; tapestry, and strange furniture that might have been designed in dreams. The haggard aspect of the little old man was wonderfully suited to the place; he might have groped among old churches and tombs, and deserted houses, and gathered all the spoils with his own hands. There was nothing in the whole collection but was in keeping with himself; nothing that looked older or more worn than he.

As he turned the key in the lock, he surveyed me with some astonishment, which was not diminished when he looked from me to my companion. The door being opened, the child addressed him as her grandfather, and told him the little story of our companionship.

'Why bless thee, child,' said the old man, patting her on the head, 'how couldst thou miss thy way? What if I had lost thee, Nell!'

'I would have found my way back to *you*, grandfather,' said the child boldly: 'never fear.'

The old man kissed her; then turned to me and begged me to walk in. I did so. The door was closed and locked. Preceding me with the light, he led me through the place I had already seen from without, into a small sitting-room behind, in which was another door opening into a kind of closet, where I saw a little bed that a fairy might have slept in: it looked so very small and was so prettily arranged. The child took a candle and tripped into this little room, leaving the old man and me together.

'You must be tired, sir,' said he as he placed a chair near the fire, 'how can I thank you?'

'By taking more care of your grandchild another time, my good friend,' I replied.

'More care!' said the old man in a shrill voice, 'more care of Nelly! why who ever loved a child as I love Nell?'

He said this with such evident surprise, that I was perplexed what answer to make; the more so, because coupled with something feeble and wandering in his manner, there were, in his face, marks of deep and anxious thought which convinced me that he could not be, as I had been at first inclined to suppose, in a state of dotage or imbecility.

'I don't think you consider –' I began. 'I don't consider!' cried the old man interrupting me, 'I don't consider her! ah, how little you know of the truth! Little Nelly, little Nelly!'

It would be impossible for any man – I care not what his form of speech might be – to express more affection than the dealer in curiosities did, in these four words. I waited for him to speak again, but he rested his chin upon his hand, and shaking his head twice or thrice, fixed his eyes upon the fire.

While we were sitting thus, in silence, the door of the closet opened, and the child returned; her light brown hair hanging loose about her neck, and her face flushed with the haste she had made to rejoin us. She busied herself, immediately, in preparing supper. While she was thus engaged I remarked that the old man took an opportunity of observing me more closely than he had done yet. I was surprised to see, that, all this time, everything was done by the child, and that there appeared to be no other persons but ourselves in the house. I took advantage of a moment when she was absent to venture a hint on this point, to which the old man replied that there were few grown persons as trustworthy or as careful as she.

'It always grieves me,' I observed, roused by what I took to be his selfishness: 'it always grieves me to contemplate the initiation of children into the ways of life, when they are scarcely more than infants. It checks their confidence and simplicity – two of the best qualities that Heaven gives them – and demands that they share our sorrows before they are capable of entering into our enjoyments.'

'It will never check hers,' said the old man, looking steadily at me, 'the springs are too deep. Besides, the children of the poor know but few pleasures. Even the cheap delights of childhood must be bought and paid for.'

'But – forgive me for saying this – you are surely not so very poor' – said I.

'She is not my child, sir,' returned the old man. 'Her mother was, and she was poor. I save nothing – not a penny – though I live as you see, but' – he laid his hand upon my arm and leant forward to whisper – 'she shall be rich one of these days, and a fine lady. Don't you think ill of me, because I use her help. She gives it cheerfully as you see, and it would break her heart if she knew that I suffered anybody else to do for me what her little hands could undertake. I don't consider!' he cried with sudden querulousness, 'why, God knows that this one child is the thought and object of my life, and yet he never prospers me – no, never!'

At this juncture, the subject of our conversation again returned, and the old man motioning to me to approach the table, broke off, and said no more.

We had scarcely begun our repast when there was a knock at the door by which I had entered; and Nell, bursting into a hearty laugh, which I was rejoiced to hear, for it was childlike and full of hilarity, said it was no doubt dear old Kit come back at last.

'Foolish Nell!' said the old man, fondling with her hair. 'She always laughs at poor Kit.'

The child laughed again more heartily than before and I could not help smiling from pure sympathy. The little old man took up a candle and went to open the door. When he came back, Kit was at his heels.

Kit was a shock-headed shambling awkward lad with an uncommonly wide mouth, very red cheeks, a turned-up nose, and certainly the most comical expression of face I ever saw. He stopped short at the door on seeing a stranger, twirled in his hand a perfectly round old hat without any vestige of a brim, and, resting himself now on one leg, and now on the other, and changing them constantly, stood in the doorway, looking into the parlour with the most extraordinary leer I ever beheld. I entertained a grateful feeling towards the boy from that minute, for I felt that he was the comedy of the child's life.

'A long way, wasn't it, Kit?' said the little old man.

'Why then, it was a goodish stretch, master,' returned Kit.

'Did you find the house easily?'

'Why then, not over and above easy, master,' said Kit.

'Of course you have come back hungry?'

'Why then, I do consider myself rather so, master,' was the answer.

The lad had a remarkable manner of standing sideways as he spoke, and thrusting his head forward over his shoulder, as if he could not get at his voice without that accompanying action. I think he would have amused one anywhere, but the child's exquisite enjoyment of his oddity, and the relief it was to find that there was something she associated with merriment, in a place that appeared so unsuited to her, were quite irresistible. It was a great point too, that Kit himself was flattered by the sensation he created, and after sev-eral efforts to preserve his gravity, burst into a loud roar, and so stood with his mouth wide open and his eyes nearly shut, laughing violently.

The old man had again relapsed into his former abstraction and took no notice of what passed; but I remarked that when her laugh was over, the child's bright eyes were dimmed with tears, called forth by the fulness of heart with which she welcomed her uncouth favourite after the little anxiety of the night. As for Kit himself (whose laugh had been all the time one of that sort which very little would change into a cry) he carried a large slice of bread and meat, and a mug of beer, into a corner, and applied himself to disposing of them with great voracity.

'Ah!' said the old man, turning to me with a sigh as if I had spoken to him but that moment, 'you don't know what you say, when you tell me that I don't consider her.'

'You must not attach too great weight to a remark founded on first appearances, my friend,' said I.

'No,' returned the old man thoughtfully, 'no. Come hither, Nell.'

The little girl hastened from her seat, and put her arm about his neck.

'Do I love thee, Nell?' said he. 'Say; do I love thee, Nell, or no?'

The child only answered by her caresses, and laid her head upon his breast.

'Why dost thou sob?' said the grandfather, pressing her closer to him and glancing towards me. 'Is it because thou know'st I love thee, and dost not like that I should seem to doubt it by my question? Well, well – then let us say I love thee dearly.'

'Indeed, indeed you do,' replied the child with great earnestness, 'Kit knows you do.'

Kit, who in despatching his bread and meat had been swallowing two-thirds of his knife at every mouthful with the coolness of a juggler, stopped short in his operations on being thus appealed to, and bawled 'Nobody isn't such a fool as to say he doesn't,' after which he incapacitated himself for further conversation by taking a most prodigious sandwich at one bite.

'She is poor now,' said the old man, patting the child's cheek, 'but, I say again, the time is coming when she shall be rich. It has been a long time coming, but it must come at last; a very long time, but it surely must come. It has come to other men who do nothing but waste and riot. When *will* it come to me!'

'I am very happy as I am, grandfather,' said the child.

'Tush, tush!' returned the old man, 'thou dost not know – how should'st thou!' Then he muttered again between his teeth, 'The time must come, I am very sure it must. It will be all the better for coming late;' and then he sighed and fell into his former musing state, and still holding the child between his knees appeared to be insensible to everything around him. By this time it wanted but a few minutes of midnight, and I rose to go.

DORIS LESSING (1919–)

Flight

*Doris Lessing spent her childhood from the age of five on a
large farm in Zimbabwe. She came to Britain, where she
lives now, in 1949. Africa provides the background for many
of her books and stories, as it does for this one.*

Above the old man's head was the dovecote, a tall wire-
netted shelf on stilts, full of strutting, preening birds. The
sunlight broke on their grey breasts into small rainbows. His
ears were lulled by their crooning, his hands stretched up
towards his favourite, a homing pigeon, a young plump
bodied bird which stood still when it saw him and cocked a
shrewd bright eye.

'Pretty, pretty, pretty,' he said, as he grasped the bird
and drew it down, feeling the cold coral claws tighten
around his finger. Content, he rested the bird lightly on his
chest, and leaned against a tree, gazing out beyond the dovecote into the landscape of a late afternoon. In folds and
hollows of sunlight and shade, the dark red soil, which was
broken into great clods, stretched wide to a tall horizon.
Trees marked the course of the valley; a stream of rich green
grass the road.

His eyes travelled homewards along this road until he
saw his granddaughter swinging on the gate underneath a
frangipani tree. Her hair fell down her back in a wave of sunlight, and her long bare legs repeated the angles of the
frangipani stems, bare, shining-brown stems among patterns of pale blossoms.

She was gazing past the pink flowers, past the railway

cottage where they lived, along the road to the village.

His mood shifted. He deliberately held out his wrist for the bird to take flight, and caught it again at the moment it spread its wings. He felt the plump shape strive and strain under his fingers; and, in a sudden access of troubled spite, shut the bird into a small box and fastened the bolt. 'Now you stay there,' he muttered; and turned his back on the shelf of birds. He moved warily along the hedge, stalking his granddaughter, who was now looped over the gate, her head loose on her arms, singing. The light happy sound mingled with the crooning of the birds, and his anger mounted.

'Hey!' he shouted; saw her jump, look back, and abandon the gate. Her eyes veiled themselves, and she said in a pert neutral voice: 'Hello, Grandad.' Politely she moved towards him, after a lingering backward glance at the road.

'Waiting for Steven, hey?' he said, his fingers curling like claws into his palm.

'Any objection?' she asked lightly, refusing to look at him.

He confronted her, his eyes narrowed, shoulders hunched, tight in a hard knot of pain which included the preening birds, the sunlight, the flowers, herself. He said: 'Think you're old enough to go courting, hey?'

The girl tossed her head at the old-fashioned phrase and sulked, 'Oh, Grandad!'

'Think you want to leave home, hey? Think you can go running around the fields at night?'

Her smile made him see her, as he had every evening of this warm end-of-summer month, swinging hand in hand along the road to the village with that red-handed, red-throated, violent-bodied youth, the son of the postmaster. Misery went to his head and he shouted angrily: 'I'll tell your mother!'

'Tell away!' she said, laughing, and went back to the gate.

He heard her singing, for him to hear:

'I've got you under my skin,
I've got you deep in the heart of . . .'

'Rubbish,' he shouted. 'Rubbish. Impudent little bit of rubbish!'

Growling under his breath he turned towards the dove-cote, which was his refuge from the house he shared with his daughter and her husband and their children. But now the house would be empty. Gone all the young girls with their laughter and their squabbling and their teasing. He would be left, uncherished and alone, with that square-fronted, calm-eyed woman, his daughter.

He stooped, muttering, before the dovecote, resenting the absorbed cooing birds. From the gate the girl shouted: 'Go and tell! Go on, what are you waiting for?'

Obstinately he made his way to the house, with quick, pathetic persistent glances of appeal back at her. But she never looked around. Her defiant but anxious young body stung him into love and repentance. He stopped. 'But I never meant . . .' he muttered, waiting for her to turn and run to him. 'I didn't mean . . .'

She did not turn. She had forgotten him. Along the road came the young man Steven, with something in his hand. A present for her? The old man stiffened as he watched the gate swing back, and the couple embrace. In the brittle shadows of the frangipani tree his granddaughter, his darling, lay in the arms of the postmaster's son, and her hair flowed back over his shoulder.

'I see you!' shouted the old man spitefully. They did not move. He stumped into the little whitewashed house, hearing the wooden veranda creak angrily under his feet. His daughter was sewing in the front room, threading a needle held to the light. He stopped again, looking back into the garden. The couple were now sauntering among the bushes, laughing. As he watched he saw the girl escape from the youth with a sudden mischievous movement, and run off through the flowers with him in pursuit. He heard shouts, laughter, a scream, silence.

'But it's not like that at all,' he muttered miserably. 'It's not like that. Why can't you see? Running and giggling, and kissing and kissing. You'll come to something quite different.'

He looked at his daughter with sardonic hatred, hating himself. They were caught and finished, both of them, but the girl was still running free.

'Can't you *see*?' he demanded of his invisible granddaughter, who was at that moment lying in the thick green grass with the postmaster's son.

His daughter looked at him and her eyebrows went up in tired forbearance.

'Put your birds to bed?' she asked, humouring him.

'Lucy,' he said urgently. 'Lucy . . .'

'Well, what is it now?'

'She's in the garden with Steven.'

'Now you just sit down and have your tea.'

He stumped his feet alternately, thump, thump, on the hollow wooden floor and shouted: 'She'll marry him. I'm telling you, she'll be marrying him next!'

His daughter rose swiftly, brought him a cup, set him a plate.

'I don't want any tea. I don't want it, I tell you.'

'Now, now,' she crooned. 'What's wrong with it? Why not?'

'She's eighteen. Eighteen!'

'I was married at seventeen and I never regretted it.'

'Liar,' he said. 'Liar. Then you should regret it. Why do you make your girls marry? It's you who do it. What do you do it for? Why?'

'The other three have done fine. They've three fine husbands. Why not Alice?'

'She's the last,' he mourned. 'Can't we keep her a bit longer?'

'Come, now, Dad. She'll be down the road, that's all. She'll be here every day to see you.'

'But it's not the same.' He thought of the other three girls, transformed inside a few months from charming petulant spoiled children into serious young matrons.

'You never did like it when we married,' she said. 'Why not? Every time, it's the same. When I got married you made me feel like it was something wrong. And my girls the same. You get them all crying and miserable the way you go on. Leave Alice alone. She's happy.' She sighed, letting her eyes linger on the sunlit garden. 'She'll marry next month. There's no reason to wait.'

'You've said they can marry?' he said incredulously.

'Yes, Dad, why not?' she said coldly, and took up her sewing.

His eyes stung, and he went out on to the veranda. Wet spread down over his chin and he took out a handkerchief and mopped his whole face. The garden was empty.

From around a corner came the young couple; but their faces were no longer set against him. On the wrist of the postmaster's son balanced a young pigeon, the light gleaming on its breast.

'For me?' said the old man, letting the drops shake off his chin. 'For me?'

'Do you like it?' The girl grabbed his hand and swung on it. 'It's for you, Grandad. Steven brought it for you.' They hung about him, affectionate, concerned, trying to charm away his wet eyes and his misery. They took his arms and directed him to the shelf of birds, one on each side, enclosing him, petting him, saying wordlessly that nothing would be changed, nothing could change, and that they would be with him always. The bird was proof of it, they said, from their lying happy eyes, as they thrust it on him. 'There, Grandad, it's yours. It's for you.'

They watched him as he held it on his wrist, stroking its soft, sun-warmed back, watching the wings lift and balance.

'You must shut it up for a bit,' said the girl intimately. 'Until it knows this is its home.'

'Teach your grandmother to suck eggs,' growled the old man.

Released by his half-deliberate anger, they fell back, laughing at him. 'We're glad you like it.' They moved off, now serious and full of purpose, to the gate, where they hung, backs to him, talking quietly. More than anything could their grown-up seriousness shut him out, making him alone; also, it quietened him, took the sting out of their tumbling like puppies on the grass. They had forgotten him again. Well, so they should, the old man reassured himself, feeling his throat clotted with tears, his lips trembling. He held the new bird to his face, for the caress of its silken feathers. Then he shut it in a box and took out his favourite.

'*Now* you can go,' he said aloud. He held it poised, ready for flight, while he looked down the garden towards the boy and the girl. Then, clenched in the pain of loss, he lifted the bird on his wrist and watched it soar. A whirr and a spatter of wings, and a cloud of birds rose into the evening from the dovecote.

At the gate Alice and Steven forgot their talk and watched the birds.

On the veranda, that woman, his daughter, stood gazing,

her eyes shaded with a hand that still held her sewing.

It seemed to the old man that the whole afternoon had stilled to watch his gesture of self-command, that even the leaves of the trees had stopped shaking.

Dry-eyed and calm, he let his hands fall to his sides and stood erect, staring up into the sky.

The cloud of shining silver birds flew up and up, with a shrill cleaving of wings, over the dark ploughed land and the darker belts of trees and the bright folds of grass, until they floated high in the sunlight, like a cloud of motes of dust.

They wheeled in a wide circle, tilting their wings so there was flash after flash of light, and one after another they dropped from the sunshine of the upper sky to shadow, one after another, returning to the shadowed earth over trees and grass and field, returning to the valley and the shelter of night.

The garden was all a fluster and a flurry of returning birds. Then silence, and the sky was empty.

The old man turned, slowly, taking his time; he lifted his eyes to smile proudly down the garden at his granddaughter. She was staring at him. She did not smile. She was wide-eyed, and pale in the cold shadow, and he saw the tears run shivering off her face.

JOHN STORTON (1909–)

A Grandad's Wishes

John Storton was brought up in the village of Cople, near Bedford, where he worked on the land. He wrote a history of his village after he had retired. This poem was included in Times Past, Poems by Ancient Britons, *a collection written by retired people in Bedford and published to celebrate the Year of the Older Person in 1993.*

A little girl said, 'Grandad, suppose
    your ship came home
And all you wished for you could buy,
    and where you wished you'd roam,
What would you spend your fortune
    on and whither would you fly?'
Said Grandad, 'That's not easy
    to answer but I'll try.
How much then will it cost me
    to hear a blackbird sing?
How much to see the snowdrops
    and the crocuses in the spring?
What price the dew upon the rose?
    To feel the summer rain?
Or walk with Grandma 'neath the
    trees along a country lane?
How much to walk a river bank and
    see a boat drift by?
Or watch the rain and sunshine paint
    a rainbow in the sky?

How much to watch a butterfly dance
    from flower to flower?
Or hear the church bell ringing to
    mark the vagrant hour?
See cobwebs in the hedgerows,
    sparkling in the rain
Like a magic carpet men would try
    to reproduce in vain?
How much to see your children grow
    and you've done the best you can,
Your little girl's a woman now and
    your son's become a man?
So what's left on my crock of gold?
    Why, goodness me
I have not spent a penny, lass; the
    things I love are free!'

from

The Forsyte Saga

*Loneliness and a yearning to see his son, young Jolyon, has
driven old Jolyon Forsyte to call on him. There has been a rift
between the two ever since young Jolyon abandoned his first
wife and daughter, June, to go and live with another woman,
whom he later married and by whom he has had two children
(the eldest being born out of wedlock). Old Jolyon meanwhile
has taken June to live in his house; and it is her increasing
preocccupation with her own life and detachment from her
grandfather that has pushed him to visit his son.*

And so that afternoon he took this journey through St John's
Wood, in the gold light that sprinkled the rounded green
bushes of the acacias before the little houses, in the summer
sunshine that seemed holding a revel over the little gardens;
and he looked about him with interest; for this was a district
which no Forsyte entered without open disapproval and
secret curiosity.

His cab stopped in front of a small house of that peculiar
buff colour which implies a long immunity from paint. It
had an outer gate, and a rustic approach.

He stepped out, his bearing extremely composed; his
massive head, with its drooping moustache and wings of
white hair, very upright, under an excessively large top hat;
his glance firm, a little angry. . . .

'Mrs Jolyon Forsyte at home?'

'Oh, yes, sir! – what name shall I say, if you please, sir?'

Old Jolyon could not help twinkling at the little maid as he gave his name. She seemed to him such a funny little toad!

And he followed her through the dark hall, into a small double drawing-room, where the furniture was covered in chintz, and the little maid placed him in a chair.

'They're all in the garden, sir; if you'll kindly take a seat, I'll tell them.'

Old Jolyon sat down in the chintz-covered chair, and looked around him. The whole place seemed to him, as he would have expressed it, pokey; there was a certain – he could not tell exactly what – air of shabbiness, or rather of making two ends meet, about everything. As far as he could see, not a single piece of furniture was worth a five-pound note. The walls, distempered rather a long time ago, were decorated with water-colour sketches; across the ceiling meandered a long crack.

These little houses were all old, second-rate concerns; he should hope the rent was under a hundred a year; it hurt him more than he could have said, to think of a Forsyte – his own son – living in such a place.

The little maid came back. Would he please to go down into the garden?

Old Jolyon marched out through the French windows. In descending the steps he noticed that they wanted painting.

Young Jolyon, his wife, his two children, and his dog Balthasar, were all out there under a pear-tree.

This walk towards them was the most courageous act of old Jolyon's life; but no muscle of his face moved, no nervous gesture betrayed him. He kept his deep-set eyes steadily on the enemy. . . .

The dog Balthasar sniffed round the edges of his trousers; this friendly and cynical mongrel – offspring of a liaison between a Russian poodle and a fox-terrier – had a nose for the unusual.

The strange greetings over, old Jolyon seated himself in a wicker chair, and his two grandchildren, one on each side of his knees, looked at him silently, never having seen so old a man.

They were unlike, as though recognising the difference set between them by the circumstances of their births. Jolly, the child of sin, pudgy-faced, with his tow-coloured hair brushed off his forehead, and a dimple in his chin, had an air of stubborn amiability, and the eyes of a Forsyte; little Holly, the child of wedlock, was a dark-skinned, solemn soul, with her mother's grey and wistful eyes.

The dog Balthasar, having walked round the three small flower-beds, to show his extreme contempt for things at large, had also taken a seat in front of old Jolyon, and oscillating a tail curled by Nature tightly over his back, was staring up with eyes that did not blink.

Even in the garden, that sense of things being pokey haunted old Jolyon; the wicker chair creaked under his weight; the garden-beds looked 'daverdy'; on the far side, under the smut-stained wall, cats had made a path.

While he and his grandchildren thus regarded each other with the peculiar scrutiny, curious yet trustful, that passes between the very young and the very old, young Jolyon watched his wife.

The colour had deepened in her thin, oval face, with its straight brows, and large grey eyes. Her hair, brushed in fine, high curves back from her forehead, was going grey, like his own, and this greyness made the sudden vivid colour in her cheeks painfully pathetic.

The look on her face, such as he had never seen there before, such as she had always hidden from him, was full of secret resentments, and longings, and fears. Her eyes, under their twitching brows, stared painfully. And she was silent.

Jolly alone sustained the conversation; he had many possessions, and was anxious that his unknown friend with extremely large moustaches, and hands all covered with blue veins, who sat with legs crossed like his own father (a habit he was himself trying to acquire), should know it; but being a Forsyte, though not yet quite eight years old, he made no mention of the thing at the moment dearest to his heart – a camp of soldiers in a shop-window, which his father had promised to buy. No doubt it seemed to him too precious; a tempting of Providence to mention it yet.

And the sunlight played through the leaves on that little party of the three generations grouped tranquilly under the pear-tree, which had long borne no fruit.

Old Jolyon's furrowed face was reddening patchily, as old men's faces redden in the sun. He took one of Jolly's hands in his own; the boy climbed on to his knee; and little Holly, mesmerized by this sight, crept up to them; the sound of the dog Balthasar's scratching arose rhythmically.

Suddenly young Mrs Jolyon got up and hurried indoors. A minute later her husband muttered an excuse, and followed. Old Jolyon was left alone with his grandchildren.

And Nature with her quaint irony began working in him one of her strange revolutions, following her cyclic laws into the depths of his heart. And that tenderness for little children, that passion for the beginnings of life which had once made him forsake his son and follow June, now worked in him to forsake June and follow these littler things. Youth, like a flame, burned ever in his breast, and to youth he turned, to the round little limbs, so reckless, that wanted care, to the small round faces so unreasonably solemn or bright, to the treble tongues, and the shrill, chuckling laughter, to the insistent tugging hands, and the feel of small bodies against his legs, to all that was young and young, and once more young. And his eyes grew soft, his voice, and thin, veined hands soft, and soft his heart within him. And to those small creatures he became at once a place of pleasure, a place where they were secure, and could talk and laugh and play; till, like sunshine, there radiated from old Jolyon's wicker chair the perfect gaiety of three hearts.

A Visit to Grandpa's

This story is in fact an account not of Dylan Thomas' grand-father but of his great grandfather, whom he never knew. David John Thomas, the poet's father, was a brilliant man, a lover of stories and poetry (he read Shakespeare aloud to his son before the child could speak). This fictionalised account of the old grandfather, transmogrified across a generation, bears witness to the father's powers of storytelling as well as to the son's imagination.

In the middle of the night I woke from a dream full of whips and lariats as long as serpents, and runaway coaches on mountain passes, and wide, windy gallops over cactus fields, and I heard the man in the next room crying, 'Gee-up!' and 'Whoa!' and trotting his tongue on the roof of his mouth.

It was the first time I had stayed in grandpa's house. The floorboards had squeaked like mice as I climbed into bed, and the mice between the walls had creaked like wood as though another visitor was walking on them. It was a mild summer night, but curtains had flapped and branches beaten against the window. I had pulled the sheets over my head, and soon was roaring and riding in a book.

'Whoa there, my beauties!' cried grandpa. His voice sounded very young and loud, and his tongue had powerful hooves, and he made his bedroom into a great meadow. I thought I would see if he was ill, or had set his bedclothes on fire, for my mother had said that he lit his pipe under the blankets, and had warned me to run to his help if I smelt smoke in the night. I went on tiptoe through the darkness to his bedroom door, brushing against the furniture and upsetting a candlestick with a thump. When I saw there was a light in the room I felt frightened, and as I opened the door I heard grandpa shout, 'Gee-up!' as loudly as a bull with a megaphone.

He was sitting straight up in bed and rocking from side to side as though the bed were on a rough road; the knotted edges of the counterpane were his reins; his invisible horse stood in a shadow beyond the bedside candle. Over a white flannel nightshirt he was wearing a red waistcoat with walnut-sized brass buttons. The over-filled bowl of his pipe smouldered among his whiskers like a little, burning hayrick on a stick. At the sight of me, his hands dropped from the reins and lay blue and quiet, the bed stopped still on a level road, he muffled his tongue into silence, and the horses drew softly up.

'Is there anything the matter, grandpa?' I asked, though the clothes were not on fire. His face in the candlelight looked like a ragged quilt pinned upright on the black air and patched all over with goat-beards.

He stared at me mildly. Then he blew down his pipe, scattering the sparks and making a high, wet dog-whistle of the stem, and shouted: 'Ask no questions.'

After a pause, he said slyly: 'Do you ever have nightmares, boy?'

I said: 'No.'

'Oh, yes, you do,' he said.

I said I was woken by a voice that was shouting to horses.

'What did I tell you?' he said. 'You eat too much. Who ever heard of horses in a bedroom?'

He fumbled under his pillow, brought out a small tinkling bag, and carefully untied its strings. He put a sovereign in my hand, and said: 'Buy a cake.' I thanked him and wished him good night.

As I closed my bedroom door, I heard his voice crying loudly and gaily, 'Gee-up! gee-up!' and the rocking of the travelling bed.

In the morning I woke from a dream of fiery horses on a plain that was littered with furniture, and of large, cloudy men who rode six horses at a time and whipped them with burning bedclothes. Grandpa was at breakfast, dressed in deep black. After breakfast he said, 'There was a terrible loud wind last night,' and sat in his arm-chair by the hearth to make clay balls for the fire. Later in the morning he took me for a walk, through Johnstown village and into the fields on the Llanstephan road.

A man with a whippet said, 'There's a nice morning, Mr Thomas,' and when he had gone, leanly as his dog, into the short-treed green wood he should not have entered because of the notices, grandpa said: 'There, do you hear what he called you? Mister!'

We passed by small cottages, and all the men who leant on the gates congratulated grandpa on the fine morning. We passed through the wood full of pigeons, and their wings broke the branches as they rushed to the tops of the trees. Among the soft, contented voices and the loud, timid flying, grandpa said, like a man calling across a field: 'If you heard those old birds in the night, you'd wake me up and say there were horses in the trees.'

We walked back slowly, for he was tired, and the lean man stalked out of the forbidden wood with a rabbit held as gently over his arm as a girl's arm in a warm sleeve.

On the last day but one of my visit I was taken to Llanstephan in a governess cart pulled by a short, weak pony. Grandpa might have been driving a bison, so tightly he held the reins, so ferociously cracked the long whip, so blasphemously shouted warning to boys who played in the road, so stoutly stood with his gaitered legs apart and cursed the demon strength and wilfulness of his tottering pony.

'Look out, boy!' he cried when we came to each corner, and pulled and tugged and jerked and sweated and waved his whip like a rubber sword. And when the pony had crept miserably round each corner, grandpa turned to me with a sighing smile: 'We weathered that one, boy.'

When we came to Llanstephan village at the top of the hill, he left the cart by the 'Edwinsford Arms' and patted the pony's muzzle and gave it sugar, saying: 'You're a weak little pony, Jim, to pull big men like us.'

He had strong beer and I had lemonade, and he paid Mrs Edwinsford with a sovereign out of the tinkling bag; she inquired after his health, and he said that Llangadock was better for the tubes. We went to look at the churchyard and the sea, and sat in the wood called the Sticks, and stood on the concert platform in the middle of the wood where visitors sang on midsummer nights and, year by year, the innocent of the village was elected mayor. Grandpa paused at the churchyard and pointed over the iron gate at the angelic headstones and the poor wooden crosses. 'There's no sense in lying there,' he said.

We journeyed back furiously: Jim was a bison again.

I woke late on my last morning, out of dreams where the Llanstephan sea carried bright sailing-boats as long as liners; and heavenly choirs in the Sticks, dressed in bards' robes and brass-buttoned waistcoats, sang in a strange Welsh to the departing sailors. Grandpa was not at breakfast; he rose early. I walked in the fields with a new sling, and shot at the Towy gulls and the rooks in the parsonage trees. A warm wind blew from the summer points of the weather; a morning mist climbed from the ground and floated among the trees and hid the noisy birds; in the mist and the wind my pebbles flew lightly up like hailstones in a world on its head. The morning passed without a bird falling.

I broke my sling and returned for the midday meal through the parson's orchard. Once, grandpa told me, the parson had bought three ducks at Carmarthen Fair and made a pond for them in the centre of the garden, but they waddled to the gutter under the crumbling doorsteps of the house, and swam and quacked there. When I reached the end of the orchard path, I looked through a hole in the hedge and saw that the parson had made a tunnel through the rockery that was between the gutter and the pond and had set up a notice in plain writing: 'This way to the pond.'

The ducks were still swimming under the steps.

Grandpa was not in the cottage. I went into the garden, but grandpa was not staring at the fruit-trees. I called across to a man who leant on a spade in the field beyond the garden hedge: 'Have you seen my grandpa this morning?'

He did not stop digging, and answered over his shoulder: 'I seen him in his fancy waistcoat.'

Griff, the barber, lived in the next cottage. I called to him through the open door: 'Mr Griff, have you seen my grandpa?'

The barber came out in his shirtsleeves.

I said: 'He's wearing his best waistcoat.' I did not know if it was important, but grandpa wore his waistcoat only in the night.

'Has grandpa been to Llanstephan?' asked Mr Griff anxiously.

'He went there yesterday in a little trap,' I said.

He hurried indoors and I heard him talking in Welsh, and he came out again with his white coat on, and he carried a striped and coloured walking-stick. He strode down the village street and I ran by his side.

When we stopped at the tailor's shop, he cried out, 'Dan!' and Dan Tailor stepped from his window where he sat like an Indian priest but wearing a derby hat. 'Dai Thomas has got his waistcoat on,' said Mr Griff, 'and he's been to Llanstephan.'

As Dan Tailor searched for his overcoat, Mr Griff was

striding on. 'Will Evans,' he called outside the carpenter's shop, 'Dai Thomas has been to Llanstephan, and he's got his waistcoat on.' 'I'll tell Morgan now,' said the carpenter's wife out of the hammering, sawing darkness of the shop.

We called at the butcher's shop and Mr Price's house, and Mr Griff repeated his message like a town crier.

We gathered together in Johnstown square. Dan Tailor had his bicycle, Mr Price his pony trap. Mr Griff, the butcher, Morgan carpenter, and I climbed into the shaking trap, and we trotted off towards Carmarthen town. The tailor led the way, ringing his bell as though there were a fire or a robbery, and an old woman by the gate of a cottage at the end of the street ran inside like a pelted hen. Another woman waved a bright handkerchief.

'Where are we going?' I asked.

Grandpa's neighbours were as solemn as old men with black hats and jackets on the outskirts of a fair. Mr Griff shook his head and mourned: 'I didn't expect this again from Dai Thomas.'

'Not after last time,' said Mr Price sadly.

We trotted on, we crept up Constitution Hill, we rattled down into Lammas Street, and the tailor still rang his bell and a dog ran, squealing, in front of his wheels. As we clip-clopped over the cobbles that led down to the Towy bridge, I remembered grandpa's nightly noisy journeys that rocked the bed and shook the walls, and I saw his gay waistcoat in a vision and his patchwork head tufted and smiling in the candlelight. The tailor before us turned round on his saddle, his bicycle wobbled and skidded. 'I see Dai Thomas!' he cried.

The trap rattled on to the bridge, and I saw grandpa there: the buttons of his waistcoat shone in the sun, he wore his tight, black Sunday trousers and a tall, dusty hat I had seen in a cupboard in the attic, and he carried an ancient bag. He bowed to us. 'Good morning, Mr Price,' he said, 'and Mr Griff and Mr Morgan and Mr Evans.' To me he said: 'Good morning, boy.'

Mr Griff pointed his coloured stick at him.

'And what do you think you are doing on Carmarthen bridge in the middle of the afternoon,' he said sternly, 'with your best waistcoat and your old hat?'

Grandpa did not answer, but inclined his face to the river wind, so that his beard was set dancing and wagging as though he talked, and watched the coracle men move, like turtles, on the shore.

Mr Griff raised his stunted barber's pole. 'And where do you think you are going,' he said, 'with your old black bag?'

Grandpa said: 'I am going to Llangadock to be buried.' And he watched the coracle shells slip into the water lightly, and the gulls complain over the fish-filled water as bitterly as Mr Price complained:

'But you aren't dead yet, Dai Thomas.'

For a moment grandpa reflected, then: 'There's no sense in lying dead in Llanstephan,' he said. 'The ground is comfy in Llangadock; you can twitch your legs without putting them in the sea.'

His neighbours moved close to him. They said: 'You aren't dead, Mr Thomas.'

'How can you be buried, then?'

'Nobody's going to bury you in Llanstephan.'

'Come on home, Mr Thomas.'

'There's a strong beer for tea.'

'And cake.'

But grandpa stood firmly on the bridge, and clutched his bag to his side, and stared at the flowing river and the sky, like a prophet who has no doubt.

Advice to His Grandson

Alex Thomas, a Nuuchah-nulth Indian from north-west Canada, recorded the advice his grandfather, Chief Tom Sayachapis, gave him in the late nineteenth century.

Don't sleep all the time. Go to bed only after having drunk water, so that you will wake up when you need to urinate. Eat once at midday, then go to sleep with [only] that much food in you so that you will not sleep soundly. As soon as everybody goes to sleep, go out and bathe [and observe rituals] . . .

Sit against the wall in the house working your mind, handling it in such a way as not to forget even one thing, that you may not wish to do evil, that you may not mock an old man, that you may not mock an old woman. Take up the orphan child who has no mother or father and say, 'Dear little fellow!' Take him to your home and feed him well so that he will think highly of you. The children to whom you do so, remember you when they grow up. Then they will help you; if you come to the beach with a canoe-load of wood, they will start unloading it for you and they will help pull the canoe up on the beach. . . . Do not make yourself important. Anyone who makes himself important is not manly. . . .

Further, let me bring to you advice as to men's things. Be a carpenter, be a maker of canoes, for you would not be manly if you had to go about the beach seeking to borrow something in which to go out to sea. Be a maker of spears and paddles; be a maker of bows and arrows; be a maker of bailers; be a maker of herring-rakes and scoop-nets for herring, for it would not be manly to lack them when you came to need things of that sort. . . .

I would say in advising her, if I had a girl, that she should also be willing to pick all kinds of berries and fruit, so that you may say to the old people 'Come and eat!' . . . If a person enters your house while you are weaving, let your work basket go. Take a good mat and have him sit on it. Don't hesitate because you happen to have clean hands. Say that you will wash your hands when you are through cooking; let him eat. When you marry into a family, look after them, so that you will likewise be looked after.

from

Advice to a Granddaughter

Letters from Queen Victoria to
Princess Victoria of Hesse

Queen Victoria, described by her grandson Kaiser Wilhelm of Prussia as 'the most unparalleled Grandmama as ever existed', kept up an intense correspondence with her granddaughter Princess Victoria. The Princess' mother, Princess Alice of Hesse, had died in the diphtheria epidemic of 1878, and Queen Victoria tried consciously to step into the role of mother to the bereaved children.

Villa Hohenlohe, Baden Baden Ap 4 1880

Darling Victoria,

May every every blessing be showered on you on your dear 17th birthday & may you have strength given you to be that support & help to your dear Papa wh he so gtly needs! Every, every where you see what your beloved Mama did . . . & you must try to follow in her footsteps – Modestly, unpresumingly, not putting yourself forward too much but being always ready to help & ready to do at Home what Papa wishes & requires.

You must learn to be posée [steady, sober], not talk too much, or too loud . . . Be always ready to listen to the advice of those whom you know to be truly devoted to you – and not those who will flatter you and wish to do what you may

like, but who often may be bad for you. My prayers for your
good will be unceasing . . .

Ever your most devoted Grandmama   VRI

*The young Victoria was also expected to keep an eye on her
siblings.*

Balmoral Oct 26 1880

I hope you, as the oldest sister will see that the younger
ones are very punctual at their lessons – for I am sorry to
say all 3 tried to evade them when they were here, & poor
Herr Müther was, with right, very much annoyed at Ernie's
laziness & constant wish to avoid his lessons . . . and he
requires to work hard & steadily now for he is very backward.

*Her grandson Ernie's 'gt. absence, inattention and backward-
ness' continued to worry the Queen and a year later she wrote:*
'He ought to go away for 2 or 3 months with Herr Müther
where he cld. have no distractions & learn steadily without
hope of picnics & expeditions wh. occupy his mind far too
much.'

Princess Victoria's future also preoccupied the Queen:

Windsor Dec 8 1880

There is another most important thing which you are quite
old enough for me to speak or write to you about. Dear
Papa, will, I know be teazed & pressed to make you marry
. . . I know full well that you (unlike, I am sorry to say, so
many Princesses abroad) – don't wish to be married for
marrying's sake and to have a position. I know darling child
that you would never do this . . . but it is a very German
view of things & I wd wish you to be prepared & on your
guard when such things are brought before Papa . . .

Write to me often & as openly as you like about
everything & it will be my greatest pleasure as well as
my greatest comfort to be of use to you.

Osborne Aug 22 1883

There is one thing wh I had wished to speak to you about, but had no opportunity of doing so, & that is: that I would earnestly warn you agst. trying to find out the reason & explanation of everything.

Science can explain many things, but there is a spiritual as well as material World and this former cannot be explained. We must have faith and trust in an all ruling, all wise & beneficent Providence . . . To try to find out the reason for everything is very dangerous & leads to nothing but disappointment & dissatisfaction, unsettling your mind & in the end making you miserable.

Though devoted to the family in Hesse (and reported to have had some of her grandchildren's milk teeth made into a bracelet), the birth of her daughter-in-law Alix's second daughter in England (the Queen's fourteenth grandchild) occasioned a rather more dismissive response:

'A very uninteresting thing – for it seems to go on like the rabbits in Windsor Park!'

MARGARET WALKER (1915–)

Lineage

Margaret Walker was born in Birmingham, Alabama. This poem was published in a collection titled For My People, *which won the Yale University Younger Poets award in 1942. She later enlarged the experiences of her great great grandmother, who lived during and after slavery, into an epic novel,* Jubilee.

My grandmothers were strong.
They followed plows and bent to toil.
They moved through fields sowing seed.
They touched earth and grain grew.
They were full of sturdiness and singing.
My grandmothers were strong.

My grandmothers are full of memories
Smelling of soap and onions and wet clay
With veins rolling roughly over quick hands
They have many clean words to say.
My grandmothers were strong.
Why am I not as they?

KATHLEEN DAYUS (1903–)

from

Her People

In Kathleen Dayus' childhood home in Birmingham in the early years of this century, children and parents lived in crowded conditions, and there was scant room for a 16-stone granny . . .

Mum's temper wasn't always at its longest first thing in the morning. She'd yell at me, 'The tea's too 'ot!' or 'It's too cold!' or 'Not enough sugar in it. You ain't stirred it up!' She'd find fault with anything. This particular morning I was saved from her nagging, but only for a short time. Just as I was about to take the mug of hot tea upstairs, a loud knock sounded on the door. I lifted the corner of the curtain and peeped out. It was only the postman, who was a cheery man with a smile for everyone he met. . . .

If only everybody in our district was as pleasant, life would have been much happier. He asked me to give a letter to Dad and returned down the yard. He'd only just stepped down from our door when Mum shouted, 'Who's that bangin' on the dower this time of the mornin'? Carn't we get any sleep around 'ere?'

She'd forgotten that she woke everybody, singing and banging at the maiding-tub at six o'clock every Monday morning.

'It's the postman, Mum. He's brought a letter for Dad,' I called back from the foot of the stairs.

I put the letter between my lips and turned to get the

mugs of tea. . . . Mum shouted down again for the letter, so I hurried up to the bedroom where I found her sitting up in bed. I put the mugs down on the cracked, marble-topped washstand and had the letter snatched from my lips.

'An' about time too!'

'It's for Dad,' I said, loud enough to wake him.

'I know, I know' she repeated. 'An' where's me tea?'

'On the table,' I answered timidly.

I made to go downstairs, but she called me back to read the letter. Mum couldn't read or write. She couldn't even count, except on her fingers and then it always took a painfully long struggle. I always did any reading or writing when Dad wasn't about. Dad could correct my spelling because he was more literate than Mum and he spoke better too. I watched him stir and yawn as I fumbled with the envelope. I was glad he was awake; it was his letter anyway. But he waved me away.

'Oh, read it, Katie, and let's get back to sleep.'

I was anxious myself now to find out what the letter contained but when I'd opened it and read it there was no extra rest for anyone that morning. It was from Granny and although her spelling was bad I managed to read it out.

'"Sam an Polly,"' I read aloud, '"I'm not well in elth me ouse as got ter be fumigated The Mans bin in an ses Ive gotter move for two weeks so Im coming ter you Ill bring wot bitta money I got an Im goin ter joyn the salvashun army an Ill bring me rocking chare an me trunk so Ill see yer all tomorra so be up early. Hannah."'

She didn't ask if she could come, she just assumed she could. When I'd finished reading the jumbled and nearly illegible writing, Mum jumped up with a start.

'Good God above!' she cried, waving her arms about. 'We ain't 'avin' 'er nuisance agen, are we?'

She glared at Dad, who was still lying on his back. He

wasn't asleep. Who could be, the way Mum was raving? But he did have his eyes closed. He was thinking about how to deal with Mum.

'Yow asleep, Sam? Dain't yer 'ear wot I said?'

'I heard yer,' he shouted back and opened his eyes wide. 'The whole bloody town can hear when you start.'

'Well, what can we do?'

'It's only for two weeks. Nobody will take her, so we'll have to do the best we can,' Dad replied.

They must have forgotten that I was still standing at the foot of the bed. I watched them both lay back again and stare up at the ceiling deep in thought. Then suddenly Mum shot up out of bed. I'd never seen her move so quickly, nor look so misshapen as she did then, standing beside the bed in her calico chemise all twisted up in the front. I'd never seen her undressed before, or without her whalebone stays. She used to have them laced so tightly she used to look like a pouter pigeon with her heavy breasts pushed up high. I never knew how she got all that flabby flesh inside those stays. She looked so comical that I had to put my hand over my mouth to keep from laughing out loud. As she leant over the bed and shook Dad, her belly wobbled and her bare breasts flopped out of the top of her chemise.

'Sam!' she shrieked. 'Wake up!'

'Stop bawling. I'm not deaf.'

'I wanta knoo where 'er's gonna sleep.'

I thought it was about time to go downstairs before they noticed me giggling.

'Shall I go and make some more hot tea, Mum?' I managed to say.

Suddenly she realised that I was still there and she yelled at me to shut up and clear off as she tried to cover herself with her shift. This was the chance I'd been waiting for, so I fled downstairs, but still strained to hear what was being said.

'Now listen, Polly, and calm down. You know she'll help. She'll bring you some money for her keep and if you don't tell the relief officer we'll be all right.'

'But where d'yer think she's gonna sleep? She carn't sleep with us. It ain't decent.'

'I'll sleep on "Neddy" for the time being so don't worry about me.'

This arrangement must have pleased her because I heard a change in her voice.

'Orl right, just as yer like, Sam.'

Now the shouting had died down, I took two mugs of tea up to find that they were still discussing Granny. I stood the mugs on the table and stood anticipating the usual grumbles from Mum but she and Dad just lay there looking snug and warm.

She pulled the clothes around her and turned to Dad.

'Do yer think the bed'll 'old us two? She's sixteen stone. I'm sixteen stone an' that meks us . . . er . . . er . . .'

I could see she was trying to puzzle out how many stones they would both be. Suddenly she sat up in bed. Sticking her two hands in front of her face and spreading her fingers apart she began to count. 'I'm sixteen and sixteen makes seventeen, eighteen, nineteen . . .'

'Sixteen and sixteen makes thirty-two,' I said, trying to help.

'I count my way then I know I'm right,' she snapped.

Dad lay back smiling and let her get on with it. Up went the fingers again and she counted on each finger again and again until eventually she yelled, 'The bed'll never 'old us!'

Dad and I collapsed in laughter as she tried with her hands to demonstrate the combined weight.

'Well,' Dad replied, still smiling, 'if you both come through the ceiling we'll have to do a moonlight flit.'

This was not the first time a flit was threatened, but we never did. . . .

Very early next morning, before anyone was awake, I heard a loud knock on the downstairs door and before I could get out of bed a louder knock and three taps on the window pane. I woke Frankie and Liza with a good hard shake and told them what was happening. We three got out of bed and dressed quickly. Then we lifted the window to see what the racket was all about. As we leant over the window sill to look down into the yard below we saw Granny at the door, calling and waving her arms in all directions.

'Ain't nobody awake yet! 'Ave I gotta stand 'ere all day? I'm freezin' an' if nobody lets me in I'm comin' through the winda.'

She sounds just like Mum, I thought. Then, before anyone could get down to let her in, she tried to push up the window. Turning to the little man who'd brought her things on a hand cart, she shouted for assistance. He looked too scared to move. Then Granny saw the bucket of rainwater that Mum kept for washing her hair. She promptly tipped the water away and turned the bucket upside down. Then she pushed the window up and stepped on to the bucket to aid her entry. The reader can imagine what a funny sight sixteen stone Granny was, standing on a rusty old bucket. We were not used to the capers that Granny cut. Suddenly, just as she was halfway through, disaster struck. The sash cord broke and the bucket slipped, leaving Granny pinned half in, half out, by the window frame. She began to kick her legs in a vain attempt to free herself but she only succeeded in showing the neighbours her pantaloons. For the first time we experienced a temper worse than Mum's. She swore till the air was blue. Proof, I thought, that she needed to join the

Salvation Army. Then Dad popped his head out of the window and called down angrily, 'You'll have to wait, Mother, while I slip me trousers on.'

When he came downstairs and saw the plight she was in, he lifted the window but he was too quick. Granny fell out backwards, rolled over the bucket and landed in a puddle of rainwater.

'An' about time too,' she bawled while he struggled to pick her off the floor.

'I'll get meself up,' she muttered.

By this time Mum's head had appeared at the window and the neighbours too were peering down at the commotion.

''Annah!' Mum shouted, 'Yer'll wake up all the neighbours.'

'Wake 'em up! Wake 'em up!' she shrieked, struggling to her feet.

She turned round and waved her fist at the amused onlookers and bellowed at them, getting redder and redder in the process.

'Look at 'em! The nosy lot of idle sods.'

All the time she'd been carrying on, the little old chap was standing still, waiting to be paid for his labours. Suddenly she turned on him, leaned against the cart and sniffed.

'Don't stand there all day. 'Elp me off with the trunk an' me rockin'-chair. An' mind 'ow yer 'andle me aspidistra.'

He couldn't manage the trunk nor the rocking-chair, but Dad soon came to the rescue. Meantime Granny felt inside the bosom of her frock, sniffed a couple of times and pushed a silver sixpence into his outstretched hand. He looked down at it disdainfully and mumbled a barely audible 'Skinny old Jew.'

'What did yer say?'

'I said, "Thank you",' he answered meekly.

'Dain't sound much like "thank yer" ter me,' she retorted.

Scratching his head, he wheeled his empty cart away, and said to Dad in a louder voice, 'I feel sorry for yow, mate,' but Dad ignored him.

The neighbours closed their windows. The fun was over for them but for us the trouble was only just beginning. We dressed hurriedly and dashed down to see Granny. She looked huge standing beside the trunk. We hadn't seen her for some time and it was easy to forget her size. She wore a black taffeta frock almost to her feet, black elastic-sided boots and a battered black woollen shawl. Her lace bonnet, also black, was hanging from ribbons on the back of her neck where it had slipped while she'd been trying to climb through the window. Her hair, too, was dishevelled, but what I noticed most was the large raised lump on her behind. I poked Frankie and he whispered, 'Ain't she got a big bum.'

'That ain't her bum. It's a bustle,' I replied as he started to snigger.

Liza too stared at Granny, but Granny paid us no attention until she suddenly straightened herself up to her full height of six feet, pulled her shawl around her and addressed us. 'Don't just stand theea gorpin'. Come an give yer ol' gran a kiss.'

I closed my eyes and lifted my face up sideways for her to kiss my cheek. She must have read my thoughts because she just pushed me roughly away, with a slap, and bent to peck Liza and Frankie's cheeks. As I walked off clutching Topsey she asked what I was holding.

'It's the golly you made me, granny,' I replied.

'I don't remember mekin' that.' She shrugged her shoulders and dismissed me.

'Now, now, Mother. You gave it to her last Christmas.

You must have forgotten.' Dad attempted to pacify her.

'Er's always forgettin',' Mum piped up from putting Granny's plant away.

'Put the kettle on, Polly, and we'll all sit down and have a cup of tea.'

This was Dad's favourite tactic when he saw a quarrel brewing. He drew Gran's rocking-chair towards the fire. Granny sat down and rocked in the creaking chair. With hers in the middle and Mum's and Dad's chairs on either side of the fireplace no one else could feel or see the flames. I picked up Topsey and sat with Frankie on 'Neddy' to await my tea. When it was made, Granny's was the first cup to be filled. Then she took a sip and without warning spat it back out.

'What yer call this?' she spluttered, pulling a face at Mum.

'It's yer tea. Like it or lump it.' This was a favourite retort.

'Tastes like maid's water ter me.' Granny could give as good as she got.

We looked at each other; we all knew what Mum's tea was like. The pot had been stewing all morning. Dad told me to make a fresh pot. As I squeezed past Mum to empty the tea leaves into the spare bucket, I heard her whisper to Dad, 'Thank the Lord we've only got 'er fer two weeks.'

JUNG CHANG (1952–)

from

Wild Swans

In 1955 Jung Chang, her sister and two brothers (aged respectively three, five, two and just over a year) were placed in nurseries after their mother had been put in detention under suspicion of working against the Chinese Communist Party. Even when their mother was released a year later she was still kept under surveillance. It was at this point that the children's grandmother came to look after them. Their father meanwhile was working as an official in the local Communist Party.

In the summer of 1956 my grandmother returned to Chengdu. The first thing she did was to rush to the nurseries and take us back to my mother's place. My grandmother had a fundamental dislike of nurseries. She said children could not be properly looked after in a group. My sister and I looked all right, but as soon as we spotted her, we screamed and demanded to go home. The two boys were another matter: Jin-ming's teacher complained that he was terribly withdrawn, and would not let any adult touch him. He only asked, quietly but obstinately, for his old nurse. My grandmother burst into tears when she saw Xiao-hei. He looked like a wooden puppet, with a meaningless grin on his face. Wherever he was put, whether sitting or standing, he would just remain there, motionless. He did not know how to ask to go to the lavatory, and did not even seem to be able to cry.

My grandmother swept him up into her arms and he instantly became her favorite.

Back at my mother's apartment, my grandmother gave vent to her anger and incomprehension. In between her tears she called my father and my mother 'heartless parents.' She did not know that my mother had no choice.

Because my grandmother could not look after all four of us, the two older ones, my sister and I, had to go to a nursery during the week. Every Monday morning, my father and his bodyguard would lift us onto their shoulders and carry us off howling, kicking, and tearing their hair.

This went on for some time. Then, subconsciously, I developed a way of protesting. I began to fall ill at the nursery, with high fevers which alarmed the doctors. As soon as I was back home, my illness miraculously evaporated. Eventually, my sister and I were allowed to stay at home.

For my grandmother, all flowers and trees, the clouds and the rain were living beings with a heart and tears and a moral sense. We would be safe if we followed the old Chinese rule for children, *ting-hua* ('heeding the words,' being obedient). Otherwise all sorts of things would happen to us. When we ate oranges my grandmother would warn us against swallowing the seeds. 'If you don't listen to me, one day you won't be able to get into the house. Every little seed is a baby orange tree, and he wants to grow up, just like you. He'll grow quietly inside your tummy, up and up, and then one day, *Ai-ya*! There he is, out from the top of your head! He'll grow leaves, and bear more oranges, and he'll become taller than our door . . .'

The thought of carrying an orange tree on my head fascinated me so much that one day I deliberately swallowed a seed – one, no more. I did not want an orchard on my head: that would be too heavy. For the whole day, I anxiously felt my skull every other minute to see whether it was still in one piece. Several times I almost asked my grandmother whether I would be allowed to eat the oranges on my head, but I checked myself so that she would not know I had been disobedient. I decided to pretend it was an accident when she saw the tree. I slept very badly that night. I felt something was pushing up against my skull.

But usually my grandmother's stories sent me happily to sleep. She had a wealth of them from classical Chinese opera. We also had a lot of books about animals and birds and myths and fairy tales. We had foreign children's stories, too, including Hans Christian Andersen and Aesop's fables. *Little Red Riding Hood*, *Snow White and the Seven Dwarfs*, and *Cinderella* were among my childhood companions.

Along with the stories, I loved nursery rhymes. They were my earliest encounters with poetry. Because the Chinese language is based on tones, its poetry has a particularly musical quality to it. I was mesmerized by my grandmother's chanting of classical poems, whose meaning I did not understand. She read them in traditional style, producing singsong, lingering sounds, rising and falling in cadence. One day my mother overheard her reciting to us some poems written in about 500 BC. My mother thought they were far too difficult for us and tried to stop her. But my grandmother insisted, saying we did not have to understand the meaning, just get the feel for the musicality of the sounds. She often said she regretted losing her zither when she left Yixian twenty years before. . . .

My grandmother was still appalled at how often my parents were absent. 'What sort of parents are these?' she would sigh, shaking her head. To make up for them, she gave all her heart and energy to us.

from

My Grandmothers and I

Diana Holman Hunt's paternal grandfather was the pre-Raphaelite painter, William Holman Hunt (1827–1910). After the early death of her mother her life was divided between her two sets of grandparents, the widow of the painter and her mother's parents. In this excerpt she is seven, and has just been hit in the eye by a tennis ball during a game on a neighbour's court. She is staying with her maternal grandmother, Mamie, and grandfather George, who is going blind. Diana's chance meeting with an ex-housemaid, Polly, who has been dismissed for becoming pregnant, prompts her to ask questions about the facts of life.

Grandmother swept into the room. 'George . . .' she began. 'Good heavens! My poor lamb, what have you done?'

'Well, what the hell has she done?' he shouted. 'Here I am, left in the dark, and you tell me nothing!' He banged his stick on the fender.

'She's got a black eye: it's horribly swollen – she's quite disfigured!' She examined me through her lorgnettes. 'Her knees are grazed, her dress is filthy – covered with stains – grass I suppose; and it looks like paint. George, can you pull the bell: twice for Fowler.'

'Damn her dress, what's happened to her eye?' He pulled the bell savagely; the cord sprang back against the wall and wriggled like a snake.

'Now my love, calm yourself; if you cry like that you will only get a red nose. Tell us what happened.'

'She was going to tell me when you came in.'

'Really George, there's no need to be offensive. Think what a shock, you shouting like that – I imagined all manner of horrors.' She held some smelling salts to her nose.

'A tennis ball hit me in the eye,' I said, aware I must avert a quarrel. . . .

'Do look at my new pocket-knife,' I said; 'although it was Sunday I bought it from Mrs. Rook's shop. I asked Lady Pritchard for the shilling.'

'You *what*?' they exclaimed in one voice. 'D'you mean you actually asked Mabel for *money*?' The atmosphere was thick with disapproval. 'Whatever possessed you to do such a thing?'

My grandmother rose from her chair, flushed with agitation. 'Surely you know you must never ask for money?'

'But I told you I wanted to buy a knife from Mrs Rook's shop.'

Grandfather stared; he too seemed interested in nothing but the shilling. 'You must never ask for money. Neither a borrower nor a lender be. Pocket-money.' He whacked his shoe with a stick. 'Mamie, perhaps she should have a regular allowance.'

'What ever for? Dear me, how very unfortunate, I must write a note to Mabel at once, Arthur can take it round before dinner.'

'She wasn't cross,' I said, smarting at their injustice, 'she has plenty of money.' . . .

Grandmother smiled to herself as she left the room to write to Lady Pritchard. They had both forgotten my eye.

'We met Polly on the drive,' I said, after a gloomy silence. 'I hadn't seen her for ages. . . . She's got terribly fat. At first I thought it was a pillow, but when I gave it a jab she said it was a baby. Did you know? I think there must be

MY GRANDMOTHERS AND I

several but she says there's only one and she's going to lay it like a hen.'

'Indeed? Quite remarkable!'

Grandfather raised his eyebrows politely.

'I know how an egg comes out but how does it get in? She doesn't seem to know.'

He said nothing, as if he hadn't heard.

'How did it get in?' I repeated, thumping a cushion in time with the words.

'I used to know,' he said at last, 'but for the moment I must confess the answer has escaped me.' He paused. 'For the life of me I cannot recollect.'

'Oh do try,' I wheedled.

'It's no good,' he said, shaking his head, 'I can't recollect, but I shouldn't ask Polly again, she might get it wrong. Mamie is younger than I am. One day perhaps she will tell you.'

'One day! What's the good of that? Why not now?'

'What a fidget you are!' As I ran from the room he called: 'Remind her, Mr. Duncan is coming at seven.'

She was sitting at her writing-table twisting the note to Lady Pritchard in a *chapeau de Napoléon* round the shilling. . . .

'I know how babies come out, I want to know how they get in. Grandfather says he's forgotten but he thinks you may remember.'

She gazed at me.

'Is that what he said?'

She picked a little mirror off the desk: 'Look at that!' she pointed at her jaw, just above the lace. 'Old age is a disaster. Who would believe I once was a beauty?'

'Yes, but what about the baby?'

Of course she was old but what did it matter?

'My love,' she sighed, gently drawing me to her, 'I have forgotten too. It is so long ago.'

'But what about the *baby*?' I insisted. 'Do try and remember!' For some reason there were tears in her eyes but she forced a smile, and whispered in my ear: 'I've lost the book of directions, yes, that's it – I've forgotten . . .'

GRACE NICHOLS (1950–)

Granny Granny Please Comb My Hair

Grace Nichols was born and grew up in Georgetown, Guyana. She came to Britain in 1977 and has published several collections of poems and children's books. The poem here comes from her book Lazy Thoughts of a Lazy Woman.

Granny Granny please comb
my hair
you always take your time
you always take such care

You put me on a cushion
between your knees
you rub a little coconut oil
parting gentle as a breeze

Mummy Mummy
she's always in a hurry-hurry
rush
she pulls my hair
sometimes she tugs

But Granny
you have all the time
in the world
and when you're finished
you always turn my head and say
'Now who's a nice girl?'

from

The Children's Grandmother

A short story writer, poet and novelist, Sylvia Townsend Warner made her name with 'Lolly Willowes', a story about a witch. Even when her theme is not the supernatural, her writing is permeated with a sense of the magic that can underlie apparent normality.

The children's grandmother was as equalitarian among my children as though she were another child. She spoke to them, even to the youngest, without a change of voice or manner, and bargained with them in such matters as winding her wool or stripping the gooseberry bushes as sternly as though they were horse dealers. They, in turn, bargained with her and, by measuring their wits against hers, came to know her as confidently as Job [the chauffeur] understood the Daimler and the tides. In spite of her threescore years and ten, she was as active as a hound. It was an extraordinary sight to see them playing hide-and-seek in the orchard – the tall old woman running, with her gray head stooped, under the lichened boughs, or folded away in some narrow hiding place, her eyes blazing with excitement. With a fickleness that matched the fickleness of a child, she would say curtly 'That's all' and walk out of the game without a trace of fatigue, for she played to please herself, not them. Even in that most grandmotherly role of storyteller, she retained an egoism of artistry. It was she who chose the stories; it was to her own ear they were addressed, or perhaps to the ghost of her unsurmisable childish self, seated among my children, who listened with critical ease to her narratives, as a cultured audience listens to a first-rate performer. 'Nothing too much.' It is, I believe, a Stoic maxim; at any rate, it is a canon of classical performance. I never heard her carried away into overdramatization or false emphasis. Her ghosts appeared without those preliminary warnings, lowered tones that say 'Here comes the ghost,' as stentorianly as the major-domo announces 'His Grace the Duke of So-and-So;' the squeals of the little pigs were related, not mimicked; her bears growled as a matter of course. Listening one evening to the dignified inflections of the Wolf Grandmother replying to the inquiries of Little Red Riding Hood, I realized that this was, in fact, the lot of my children: They had a Wolf Grandmother, a being who treated them with detached benignity, who played with them and dismissed them and enjoyed them without scruple, and would, at a pinch, defend them with uncontaminated fury. Her eyes were large the better to see them with, her ears long the better to hear them, her claws sharp the better to tear – by an accident of kinship – not them but the village of St. Keul, the malevolence of the sea, the Jesuitry of the bedtime chocolate.

Little Red-Cap

*The Grimm brothers published 'Little Red-Cap' in 1812
in their collection of folktales 'dating back to most ancient
times' (Wilhelm Grimm). The roots of this story can in fact
be traced to an eleventh-century Latin fable about a little
girl in a red cap who meets wolves. It then reappeared in
seventeenth-century France as a cautionary tale which was
translated and published in England some 50 years later. The
Grimm variant throws up some interesting questions, as
analysed by the psychologist Bruno Bettelheim in his book*
The Uses of Enchantment: *the grandmother has to be
eaten, he says, because 'grandparents must be of use to the
child . . . [must] protect him, teach him, feed him; if not,
then they're reduced to a lower form of existence'. However,
the story's happy ending, with the rescue ('rebirth') of
grandmother and granddaughter out of the dark void of the
wolf's inside, offers hope to us all: even when we've patently
failed in our duties, redemption is possible.*

Once upon a time there was a dear little girl who was loved
by every one who looked at her, but most of all by her grandmother, and there was nothing that she would not have
given to the child. Once she gave her a little cap of red velvet,
which suited her so well that she would never wear anything
else; so she was always called 'Little Red-Cap.'

One day her mother said to her: 'Come, Little Red-Cap,
here is a piece of cake and a bottle of wine; take them to your
grandmother, she is ill and weak, and they will do her good.

Set out before it gets hot, and when you are going, walk nicely and quietly and do not run off the path, or you may fall and break the bottle, and then your grandmother will get nothing; and when you go into her room, don't forget to say, "Good-morning," and don't peep into every corner before you do it.'

'I will take great care,' said Little Red-Cap to her mother, and gave her hand on it.

The grandmother lived out in the wood, half a league from the village, and just as Little Red-Cap entered the wood, a wolf met her. Red-Cap did not know what a wicked creature he was, and was not at all afraid of him.

'Good-day, Little Red-Cap,' said he.

'Thank you kindly, wolf.'

'Whither away so early, Little Red-Cap?'

'To my grandmother's.'

'What have you got in your apron?'

'Cake and wine; yesterday was baking-day, so poor sick grandmother is to have something good, to make her stronger.'

'Where does your grandmother live, Little Red-Cap?'

'A good quarter of a league farther on in the wood; her house stands under the three large oak-trees, the nut-trees are just below; you surely must know it,' replied Little Red-Cap.

The wolf thought to himself: 'What a tender young creature! what a nice plump mouthful – she will be better to eat than the old woman. I must act craftily, so as to catch both.' So he walked for a short time by the side of Little Red-Cap, and then he said: 'See, Little Red-Cap, how pretty the flowers are about here – why do you not look round? I believe, too, that you do not hear how sweetly the little birds are singing; you walk gravely along as if you were going to school, while everything else out here in the wood is merry.'

Little Red-Cap raised her eyes, and when she saw the

sunbeams dancing here and there through the trees, and pretty flowers growing everywhere, she thought: 'Suppose I take grandmother a fresh nosegay; that would please her too. It is so early in the day that I shall still get there in good time'; and so she ran from the path into the wood to look for flowers. And whenever she had picked one, she fancied that she saw a still prettier one farther on, and ran after it, and so got deeper and deeper into the wood.

Meanwhile the wolf ran straight to the grandmother's house and knocked at the door.

'Who is there?'

'Little Red-Cap,' replied the wolf. 'She is bringing cake and wine; open the door.'

'Lift the latch,' called out the grandmother, 'I am too weak, and cannot get up.'

The wolf lifted the latch, the door sprang open, and without saying a word he went straight to the grandmother's bed, and devoured her. Then he put on her clothes, dressed himself in her cap, laid himself in bed and drew the curtains.

Little Red-Cap, however, had been running about picking flowers, and when she had gathered so many that she could carry no more, she remembered her grandmother, and set out on the way to her.

She was surprised to find the cottage-door standing open, and when she went into the room, she had such a strange feeling that she said to herself: 'Oh dear! how uneasy I feel to-day, and at other times I like being with grandmother so much.' She called out: 'Good morning,' but received no answer; so she went to the bed and drew back the curtains. There lay her grandmother with her cap pulled far over her face, and looking very strange.

'Oh! grandmother,' she said, 'what big ears you have!'

'The better to hear you with, my child,' was the reply.

'But, grandmother, what big eyes you have!' she said.

'The better to see you with, my dear.'

'But, grandmother, what large hands you have!'

'The better to hug you with.'

'Oh! but, grandmother, what a terrible big mouth you have!

'The better to eat you with!'

And scarcely had the wolf said this, than with one bound he was out of bed and swallowed up Red-Cap.

When the wolf had appeased his appetite, he lay down again in the bed, fell asleep and began to snore very loud. The huntsman was just passing the house, and thought to himself: 'How the old woman is snoring! I must just see if she wants anything.' So he went into the room, and when he came to the bed, he saw that the wolf was lying in it. 'Do I find you here, you old sinner!' said he. 'I have long sought you!' Then just as he was going to fire at him, it occurred to him that the wolf might have devoured the grandmother, and that she might still be saved, so he did not fire, but took a pair of scissors, and began to cut open the stomach of the sleeping wolf. When he had made two snips, he saw the little Red-Cap shining, and then he made two snips more, and the little girl sprang out, crying: 'Ah, how frightened I have been! How dark it was inside the wolf'; and after that the aged grandmother came out alive also, but scarcely able to breathe. Red-Cap, however, quickly fetched great stones with which they filled the wolf's belly, and when he awoke, he wanted to run away, but the stones were so heavy that he collapsed at once, and fell dead.

Then all three were delighted. The huntsman drew off the wolf's skin and went home with it; the grandmother ate the cake and drank the wine which Red-Cap had brought, and revived, but Red-Cap thought to herself: 'As long as I live, I will never by myself leave the path, to run into the wood, when my mother has forbidden me to do so.'

PATSY GRAY

Grandmothers

This essay was written by a seven-year-old, Patsy Gray. It was first published in her school Parent-Teacher Association magazine.

A grandmother is a lady who has no children of her own, so she likes other people's little girls and boys. A grandfather is a male grandmother. He goes for walks with the boys and they talk about fishing and tractors.

Grandmothers don't have to do anything but be there. They are old, so they shouldn't play hard or run. They should never say 'Hurry up.' Usually they are fat, but not too fat to tie children's shoes. They wear glasses and funny underwear, and they can take their teeth and gums off. They don't have to be smart, only answer questions like why cats hate dogs and why God isn't married. They don't talk baby-talk like visitors. When they read to us they don't skip bits, or mind if it's the same story over again.

Everybody should have one, especially if you don't have television, because grandmothers are the only grownups who have time.

WALTER DE LA MARE (1873–1956)
The Cupboard

This poem comes from Walter de la Mare's collection Peacock Pie. *As in much of his verse for children, under the surface sweetness a suggestion of less comfortable realities is hinted at. One wonders how welcoming that 'slippery knee' really was.*

I know a little cupboard,
With a teeny tiny key,
And there's a jar of Lollipops
For me, me, me.

It has a little shelf, my dear,
As dark as dark can be,
And there's a dish of Banbury Cakes
For me, me, me.

I have a small fat grandmamma,
With a very slippery knee,
And she's Keeper of the Cupboard,
With the key, key, key.

And when I'm very good, my dear,
As good as good can be,
There's Banbury Cakes, and Lollipops
For me, me, me.

MARJORIE SHOSTAK

from

Nisa, the Life and Words of a !Kung Woman

Nisa, one of the !Kung tribe who live in the Kalahari Desert in south-west Africa, tells in her own words how as a child she sought protection with her grandmother from her parents' wrath. This account was published in 1981.

Another time, I was out gathering with my mother, my father, and my older brother. After a while, I said, 'Mommy, give me some klaru [edible bulbs].' She said, 'I still have to peel these. As soon as I do, we'll go back to the village and eat them.' I had also been digging klaru to take back to the village, but I ate all I could dig. My mother said, 'Are you going to eat all your klaru right now? What will you eat when you get back to the village?' I started to cry. My father told me the same, 'Don't eat all your klaru here. Leave them in your pouch and soon your pouch will be full.' But I didn't want that, 'If I put all my klaru in my pouch, which ones am I going to eat now?'

Later, I sat down in the shade of a tree while they gathered nearby. As soon as they had moved far enough away, I climbed the tree where they had left a pouch hanging, full of klaru, and stole the bulbs. I had my little pouch, the one my father had made me, and as I took the bulbs, I put them in it. I took out more and more and put them all in together. Then I climbed down and sat waiting for them to return.

They came back, 'Nisa, you ate the klaru! What do you have to say for yourself?' I said, 'Uhn, uhn, I didn't take them.' My mother said, 'So, you're afraid of your skin hurting, afraid of being hit?' I said, 'Uhn, uhn, I didn't eat those klaru.' She said, 'You *ate* them. You certainly did. Now, don't do that again! What's making you keep on stealing?'

My older brother said, 'Mother, don't punish her today. You've already hit her too many times. Just leave her alone.'

'We can see. She says she didn't steal the klaru. Well then, what did eat them? Who else was here?'

I started to cry. Mother broke off a branch and hit me, 'Don't steal! Can't you understand! I tell you, but you don't listen. Don't your ears hear when I talk to you?' I said, 'Uhn, uhn. Mommy's been making me feel bad for too long now. I'm going to stay with Grandma. Mommy keeps saying I steal things and hits me so that my skin hurts. I'm going to go stay with Grandma. I'll go where she goes and sleep beside her wherever she sleeps. And when she goes out digging klaru, I'll eat what she brings back.'

But when I went to my grandmother, she said, 'No, I can't take care of you this time. If you stay with me, you'll be hungry. I'm old and only go gathering one day in many. Most mornings I just stay around. We'll sit together and hunger will kill you. Now, go back and sit beside your mother and father.' I said, 'No, Daddy will hit me. Mommy will hit me. My skin hurts from being hit. I want to stay with you.'

I lived with her for a while. But I was still full of tears. I just cried and cried and cried. I sat with her and no matter if the sun was setting or was high in the sky, I just cried. One month, when the nearly full moon rose just after sunset, I went back to my mother's hut. I said, 'Mommy, you hate me. You always hit me. I'm going to stay on with Grandma. You hate me and hit me until I can't stand it any more. I'm tired.'

Another time when I went to my grandmother, we lived in another village, nearby. While I was there, my father said to my mother, 'Go, go bring Nisa back. Get her so she can be with me. What did she do that you chased her away from here?' When I was told they wanted me to come back I said, 'No, I won't go back. I'm not going to do what he said. I don't want to live with Mother. I want to stay with Grandma; my skin still hurts. Today, yes, this very day here, I'm going to just continue to sleep beside Grandma.'

So, I stayed with her. Then, one day she said, 'I'm going to take you back to your mother and father.' She took me to them, saying, 'Today, I'm giving Nisa back to you. But isn't there someone here who will take good care of her? You don't just hit and hit a child like this one. She likes food and likes to eat. All of you are lazy. You've just left her so she hasn't grown well. If there were still plenty of food around, I'd continue to take care of her. She'd just continue to grow up beside me. Only after she had grown up, would she leave. Because all of you have killed this child with hunger. With your own fingers you've beaten her, beaten her as though she weren't a Zhun/twa.* She was always crying. Look at her now, how small she still is.' But my mother said, 'No, listen to me. Your little granddaughter . . . whenever she saw food with her eyes, she'd just start crying.'

Oh, but my heart was happy! Grandmother was scolding Mother! I held so much happiness in my heart that I laughed and laughed. But when Grandmother went home and left me there I cried and cried. My father yelled at me, but he didn't hit me. His anger usually came out only from his mouth. 'You're so senseless! Don't you realize that after you left, everything felt less important? We wanted you to be with us. Yes, even your mother wanted you and missed you.

* Zhun/twaso: name !Kung use for themselves, from *Zhu* meaning person and /*twa* meaning 'true or real'.

Today, everything will be all right when you stay with us. Your mother will take you where she goes; the two of you will do things together and go gathering together. Why do you refuse to leave your grandmother now?'

But I cried and cried. I didn't want to leave her. 'Mommy, let me go back and stay with Grandma, let me follow after her.' But my father said, 'That's enough. No more talk like that. There's nothing here that will hit you. Now, be quiet.' And I was quiet. After that, when my father dug klaru bulbs, I ate them, and when he dug chon bulbs, I ate them. I ate everything they gave me, and I wasn't yelled at any more.

SALIM HAKIM (1931–)

from

Grandma and I

This excerpt from a longer fictionalised account of his grand-mother evokes Salim Hakim's early life in a large Iraqi family, where the children were often put into the charge of the senior female members of the clan.

The two Imams of the Azbakia Mosque and the Sabonjia Mosque persistently undercut each other's izzan, the call for prayer, by a few minutes each time so as to be the early bird which catches the worm, so to speak.

'I can no longer know whether this is the sunset izzan or the afternoon izzan,' Grandma lamented with anger as the process of time rolling continued. 'We'll soon have the evening prayers said at noon time and the noon prayers at dawn.'

Losing faith in the call of minarets, Grandma bought a second-hand chiming clock from Suq al Haraj and hung it on one of the two wooden hexagonal pillars shouldering the ceiling of the arabesque decorated iwan, the spacious living alcove opening on the haush, the central courtyard. Instead of raising her eyes to heaven through the open haush and piously murmuring 'God is greater' every time the izzan was heard from the minaret, she started to utter the most honoured words whenever the German clock chimed the correct hour, or, more precisely, what went for the correct hour; for Grandma was illiterate and could not read the face of the clock, which left her with no option but to rely on counting the number of its strikes. 'Shush!' was immediately pronounced as the slightest move from the old clock was heard, signalling to the women to start counting: one, two, three and so on. Of course, once it stopped they had no means of starting the clock correctly, which left me with the proud function of getting it going again. An argument usually followed among the four women who inhabited the house: Grandma, her deaf sister and her two daughters, all widows of diverse wars and insurrections long forgotten by the people who had fought them. Arguing among themselves on the flimsiest topic was the only form of entertainment they could devise, and the time for prayer was the favourite occasion for such arguments. Who needed an ablution, was it early for the afternoon prayer or too late for the noon prayer, did Auntie Salima do the morning worship twice by mistake or was that Auntie Zaynab who sulked and prayed in the kitchen? Who slept during the sacred duty, who broke wind and needed another ablution? Such were the questions of the day, but whatever they did and however they argued, agreed or disagreed, they never prayed together. The German clock started a new topic for disputation. Was it proper to say 'God is greater' after the chiming of a devilish machine of infidel manufacture, or should they say those words only after the proper izzan from the mosque?

Dressed in black from the neck to the ankles and with their grey hair wrapped in black futas, they sat in the iwan all day long, each in her own corner, hailing the names of God silently with the help of their black rosaries, their trembling lips faintly moving like the mouths of fishes just out of water. The colour of the rosary beads, jet black, did not help in maintaining peace and tranquillity in the house, for the old women, their sight already in decline, often mistook one rosary for another which invariably ended in a heated argument between Auntie Salima and Auntie

Zaynab or between them and Grandma or any combination of the four, for that matter.

'How many times did I say to you specifically not to use my rosary?'

'What difference does it make? It is all in praise of God.'

'You are saying that again, you grey haired old woman, and I told you a thousand times that my rosary has been to Mecca and gone round the grave of the Prophet, peace be upon him. Yours hasn't been anywhere. Yours is only a cheap string of beads bought from Suq al Haraj!'

The arguments went on and on with a great deal of resentment and rage until the next call for prayer was heard. I listened, and wondered whether it was not the work of the devil himself that all the four women had bought rosaries in black and no other colour.

HELENA NORBERG-HODGE

from

Ancient Futures: Learning from Ladakh

When the author first met the grandmother, Abi-le, in the village house in Ladakh in the Himalayas where she stayed, she found her chanting a mantra, 'her hands gliding across well-worn wooden prayer beads in her lap'. Later, she watched her at her household chores. The author spent much of her time living with the Ladakhis over a period of ten years, and published this account in 1991.

Abi-le did not throw away the barley after making *chang* from it. She had already poured water over the boiled and fermented grain to make four separate brews. Then instead of discarding it, she spread the grain on a yak-hair blanket to dry so it could later be ground for eating. She molded the crushed remains of apricot kernels, a dark brown paste from which oil had already been carefully squeezed, into the form of a small cup; later, when it had hardened, she would use the cup to turn her spindles. She even saved the dishwater, with its tiny bits of food, to provide a little extra nourishment for the animals . . .

The children would inevitably run to Grandmother for consolation if they had been hurt or reprimanded. She would rock them or play with them until all was forgotten. It was Abi-le who would ask special favours on their behalf, and it was she who made tiny ibex figures out of cheese for them, stringing them into a necklace that they could nibble on.

DAPHNE GLAZER (1938–)

Phoenix Rising

Daphne Glazer is not herself a grandmother but this story is based on her observations of others. Its main character, bruised from a relationship with a younger man, sees grand- parenthood as a giant step on the road to becoming old. But the arrival of a vibrant new entity in her life is the signal for her own rebirth.

Babs knew it was going to be one of those times when she felt certain that the world was flat: she could fall off and tumble into the abyss if she didn't watch out. She felt she was drawing goosepimplingly close to it.

You'd best go back home, love. There's no sense in you waiting around here, the nurse had said. We'll give you a ring when it's all over. The nurse had been smiling but firm. She'd also given Babs a certain thorough once-over with her eyes. Of course people always did. They expected women of her age to have become grey-permed and knitted, with shoes for the wider-foot-you-know. Their eyes said: Hm, a tart, a scarlet woman – she's knockin' on a bit for that gear! Babs had a back straight as Nelson's Column, long shaggy black hair; carefully applied tan cheeks whatever the season; ruby lips; she wore black leggings and a black leather jacket embellished with studs and black boots.

What was she going to do? There must be a café or a pub close by where she could sit for a bit. She wanted to be near Shaz and think about everything. Nothing would make her leave the vicinity of the hospital.

Mam, I'm so tired, Shaz had kept on saying. How much

more of it will there be? I never thought it'ud be like this. Her sallow face gleamed with sweat.

Then the white coats had flapped in and there was some consultation whilst Shaz lay there like some great ruined whale washed up on a bank of shingle, sides juddering with strain.

Mam, I'm frightened.

It'll be all right, love. Babs squeezed her hand. But would it? Shaz was a panicker, always had been. She couldn't bear 'biggies' – people who tried to push her about, like doctors and social workers and benefit office clerks. Shaz trailed by in long tasselled Indian skirts and little tops she'd bought in 'Cancer Research' or 'Sue Ryder'. These days Oxfam were too pricy. Her bead earrings dangled almost to her shoulders and she wore a fake diamond in her left nostril and tatty friendship bands on her wrists.

Wherever she went she spread an aura of sandalwood that hinted at Eastern bazaars and plodding camels. Her hennaed hair turned her into a bedraggled Medusa. This did not go down well in job centres, offices or in any known employment. It aroused suspicions: New Age hippie, people pronounced. She had always been out of step, right from her school days and even earlier.

Mrs Sherman, I have to tell you, your daughter has been smoking behind the lavatories.

Mrs Sherman, your daughter has been indulging in advanced sex in the school lavatories.

What was that – it sounded most interesting. French kisses, that was all.

Babs stood in the lift, expecting it to plunge to the bottom of the shaft or stop suddenly between floors and leave her gaping for oxygen. A suited middle-aged man planted himself beside her. She felt he belonged to a much older generation, though he was probably her junior. He kept on sliding glances at her which she ignored. At every floor the lift halted, the doors sished open to reveal grey shining floors and late night hospital silence.

I want to stay, she'd told the doctors.

No, Mrs Sherman, I'm afraid you can't – we don't allow visitors in during a caesarean section –

She'd been at the hospital two nights and two days whilst Shaz did her deep breathing and struggled with bands of pain and sweated and shambled about the room, trying to suppress her groans.

Periodically Babs had left her to find a phone and tell Rick, Shaz's elusive partner, how things were.

I'm sorry, Rick had said, but I can't be doin' with them places . . . can't abide bodies. They make me come out in a sweat hospitals do, like cremis . . .

Rick was right enough, Babs thought, but utterly useless. He could never bring himself to visit the dentist or the doctor. Shaz went for him to the doctor's if he happened to be ill, described his symptoms and said they were hers, which could be a bit tricky at times – particularly with problems below the belt.

The lights of a transport caff winked at her from across the main trunk road where lorries thundered day and night on their way to the docks. She'd pop across there and have a coffee and maybe beans on toast or something.

All sorts of partially submerged fragments were beginning to surface: things she hadn't really examined and didn't know that she wanted to now.

Shaz's baby had all along been a very precarious matter – would she manage it, that was the big question and for that reason Babs hadn't really let herself dwell on a baby's implications for her. When, and if ... don't let her think about if ... Shaz's baby was born that would make her a grandma: somebody's nana. Her own nana had been a big woman, bossy but kind – the sort who's slapping your legs and bawling one minute and hugging you the next and stuffing goodies-money into your hand and telling you you're a little poppet. Being with Nana had been like sitting on a sea-saw . . . plus, Nana had seemed ancient, a Darby and Joan person in an acrylic jumper and wearing a pleated skirt, or a courtelle dress and shoes with holes in like that Swiss cheese and bunion pockets. Shoes were always a give-away when you were trying to appear youthful. Seductiveness lay in feet. Doc Martens could be sexy but beige-coloured basket-weave or pocked numbers with stout lacing and hefty straps were just plain nunty. They were as fuddy as the black dresses and veiling that nanas wore in some hot countries.

She sat with a thick white mug in front of her.

'Beans comin' up, love.'

Red-necked men in demins sat at the tables, clattering cutlery on the formica and dobbing ash on plates. They coughed and barked with laughter and now and then their eyes swivelled to her and then they quickly looked away. She could imagine their comments: Thought as it was a young bird with that hair but she's not, she's a granny . . . an old bag that one . . .

She kept her head up straight and wouldn't look at them.

It had been a traumatic year because of Darran. Nobody really knew how that hurt. He'd shared her bed for ten years and now he'd gone . . . She'd met him at the Dance Studio and he'd stood peeking at her whilst she did a work out in her shiny black leotards.

Hi, he'd said, you dance real well . . .

Ta.

He was a kid and she'd taken no more notice: a blond, square-jawed kid, neat little body, just her height; the sort with earnest, blazing blue eyes. There was a point when you had to school yourself not to take these young kids seriously. Once upon a time that would have been the right season for you, but it no longer was. He must have been twenty-one then.

'Beans, love!' the sweating middle-aged woman behind the counter called. The tops of her arms jellied as she moved. She'll be my age, Babs registered, is she a grandma? How old would her grandkids be? Yes, she looked like Nana, that was her role . . . but nanas sat at home minding the grandbairns and watched telly or shambled out to bingo; they weren't in paid work. Though maybe only nanas would be working at such an unsocial time in a place like this. Perhaps she was younger . . . a lot younger . . .

What could be happening to Shaz now? The trouble with doctors, they never told you where it was at and because they didn't, your imagination free-wheeled alarmingly.

We think it best to give her a caesarian section under the circumstances . . .

What circumstances?

Women still died in childbirth . . . not many nowadays, not in Britain. But they still could. There were always exceptions. You could never tell with Shaz. There was the time when she was eighteen months old and suddenly went rigid and seemed to stop breathing. Babs had phoned for an ambulance. A febrile convulsion, they said later, caused by a throat infection. It was all over so quickly, but for several hours, she'd thought of nothing else: Shaz, her little black-haired daughter, might be dying.

She mustn't think of that, but concentrating on Darran was no safer.

Darran had laid siege to her; followed her about, then they'd become ballroom dancing partners. Somehow they fitted – she so dark and he so fair. When she glided over

glassy acres of parquet in her black besequinned gown and
he had one hand on the small of her back and the other
touching her palm, they became part of the rushing and
swelling of the music, that grand drift which let them fly and
soar. Their reflections were caught in the mirrored walls and
thrown back. And she'd seen herself, a mature woman;
somebody who knew about the world, had been married
and divorced, had lovers – was a mother, a single parent, ran
a home. She'd been flaming and glowing; seen better from a
distance because of the coarsening of her texture – she'd lost
the smooth satin of youth – but the lines and the roughening
of maturity had given her something too. There he was
beside her his hair cut in a flat-top – a field of blond stubble
that she wanted to stroke, and the unformed loveliness of his
pale face. He'd been so perfect, so untouched, not lugging
with him the ball and chain of disillusionment. Love was
for ever.

Barbara, he'd said, Barbara, I think you're beautiful and
I shall always love you . . .

People stared at them when they walked down the
street, stared and muttered. It was somehow an affront to
them that this middle-aged woman should be holding the
hand of such a young man.

Toy-boy, they said and sniggered, Babs' toy-boy.

How's your toy-boy doing?

They hadn't become lovers for a long time because she
was resisting taking him seriously: he was just a kid. But then
they did, and it lasted.

At the shops acquaintances said: Is Darran still with you
then? Are you still seeing that what's-his-name? They
quizzed Shaz too: Is your Mam still with that lad? Neighbours nebbed at her from behind their nets: they were waiting for her downfall. It was bound to come.

Oh, he'll get tired of her – they do . . . they move on . . .

he's just sewing his wild oats, cutting his teeth . . . well, I mean to say, she must be old enough to be his Mam . . . well, his Nana even . . . who knows.

At first she hadn't wanted him to see her naked: the rippling of her stretch marks from the birth of Shaz; the occasional blue thread-veins on her thighs. His body was blond and hairless, his hip-bones jutted and his belly was flat and hard. His pale neck was a silky column. What a serious lad he was!

I love you for all of it, he said . . . because each crease is part of you – it's what you are.

He was shy and considerate. Bill, Shaz's father, had been big and bullying, a take-it-or-leave-it man. If she'd put her point of view then she was being argumentative, because of course there was only one answer to the question and one point of view and that was his. It had all been about being right and Bill was unfailingly right – it was important to him this rightness, whereas Babs couldn't have cared less.

They might have gone on and on – what was there to interrupt that Indian summer? Never before had she felt so conscious of each day, because it was another day with him. She'd run her dance school and won medals for ballroom dancing, and then one night, late on after a competition at Blackpool where they'd come second, he'd said:

Barbara, I er want to tell you something . . . I've been thinking.

She'd looked across the table at him, noted his high colour – he was thirty-one and that satin shine had disappeared. Why hadn't she noticed before? Instinctively she knew it was coming . . . that was the way it went: the big things took you unawares every time, like death.

Barbara . . .

Yes, she said, yes?

Barbara, I've got something to tell you.

Mm.

I've been feeling very depressed lately . . . I mean, I'm not getting anywhere . . . and I think I want an ordinary family life . . . a wife and kids . . . if I don't look sharp it'll be too late.

At the words 'kids' she'd been pulled up short, because at fifty-six they were something she couldn't give him: she was too old. It had seemed in that moment as though a shutter came down: the shutter of age. She was old and done for. None of it mattered once she'd heard the first words.

Yes, she'd said. She hadn't argued because there was no point. Perhaps her easy acceptance surprised him. Yes, you'd better go and start a new life, Darran.

So, the following weekend, crying, he left. She didn't cry not then nor later.

Babs finished her beans on toast, fastened the belt on her leather jacket and retraced her steps to the hospital. Lights still blazed in oblong windows. Trees lining the drive threw the black wires of their branches on the pale, sodium-stained sky.

She should never have left the hospital premises, she should have sat in the corridor and refused to budge. What if Shaz had died? What if the baby was malformed? There had been all that bleeding at the start and months in bed for fear of miscarriage; those scans that couldn't locate the baby's exact position . . . where was the head?

Perhaps it'll be a monster, Shaz had joked.

The nurse hadn't smiled.

Back on the ward. 'I wonder if Sharon Sherman has had her baby yet?' she asked a staff nurse.

'Oh yes, they've just delivered her.'

Babs felt her heart hopping. 'Is everything all right?' 'Fine – a little girl – eight pounds six ounces. You can go in for a minute.'

'Mam, Mam . . .' Shaz propped up on pillows was smiling, with a sort of radiance. It wasn't an ordinary smile. 'They gave me an epidural at the finish, it freezes your legs and everything. Have you seen her?'

A nurse fetched the baby for Babs' inspection.

This suddenly was another important moment. The nurse placed the white bundle in Babs' arms. She looked down at a pale composed little face with its black feathery brows and head covered with dandelion-clock hair. Somewhere she seemed to see her own mother in that face . . . Mam, dead thirty years now. Mam and Nana were both contained in that tiny body and the fathers, also long dead – all that striving, the loving and the hating and the mistakes and the triumphs were contained in this new little person.

'Well, Mam, you're a Nana now,' Shaz was saying and Babs found her eyes filling with tears of joy. It was all starting again . . . a new love affair.

As she left the hospital building on her way to the car park she remembered the sticker she had seen in the back window of a woman's car the previous day.

'I'm a grandma,' it had said, 'why couldn't I of had the grandbairns first–'

Now she understood what it meant.

NELL DUNN (1936–)

from

Grandmothers

In her interviews with 'new' grandmothers Nell Dunn came across many different reactions, but few had experienced quite the same sense of apprehension that afflicted her as she contemplated this awesome and novel relationship – until a chance encounter with strangers showed her the way.

Here was I faced with a little baby, who wasn't mine, and I saw I had to make a move to love without yet being loved. I came up against this icy, tight and calculating part of me: 'Why should I give him anything? He's not mine.' I did all the right things in the practical sense, but the love was slow in coming. Very slow.

Then one afternoon I'd taken him for a walk in the park nearby. He was about three months old . . . I was sitting on a bench in the rose garden when two Indian women came up with a little girl. They started admiring him and asked if they could hold him. It turned out they were a mother, daughter and granddaughter, and they were full of pleasure as they sat beside me on the bench, the sun glinting on their sparkling saris, and congratulated me on my immense good fortune at having a beautiful grandson. I felt very proud and then, as they handed him back, he smiled at me and I was suddenly, all at once, bowled over. Overcome, I hid my face in his warm little stomach and I knew that yes, I was immensely fortunate!

ELIZABETH CAIRNS (1933–)
Milestones

This story, which arises out of front-line experience in grand-mothering, aims to show two things: how overwhelming can be the sense of wanting to do it better this time, and how, in counterpoint to that, the experience of being a grandparent may mean very different things to the two partners in grand-parenthood.

Two's company, three's none. True or false? It all depends, you'll probably say. But in my experience, it's *always*, always true.

I'm good at one-to-ones, have been all my life. Brian and I were a one-to-one – till Life intervened. Life in various two and four legged forms (like that plague of puppies, sops for unhappy teenagers) . . . I see those years as a great swelling sea, choppy and wild, with breakers that curved over you and left you gasping for breath, then sudden calms shot through with rays of gold. Please let it last, I'd pray . . . as the next storm clouds billowed up. Brian, I knew, couldn't wait for the end. But I just thought, so long as they're happy I don't mind anything.

I'm talking, of course, about the children. The little octopuses who clung and winkled and lashed and hugged and finally, twenty years later, waved goodbye. They left, and in the silence and space that surrounded us we began to rebuild our separate and together lives. I could stand in the hall by that chest with the dried flowers (and the drying face in the mirror above them), shout 'Hullo – anyone in?' And no one was. Just an empty house, opening its arms to me.

Loneliness? Of course, there were moments. But against that, the thirst-quenching sense of myself and us. Of two people meeting after a long train journey where by some bureaucratic error they had booked places in separate compartments, continuing the journey in adjoining seats.

But it had always been there, hadn't it. The next wave, the surge just over the horizon. A biological inevitability, said Jane my wise best friend, with a role model like you. As with many age-old friends, Jane's insights were fossilised under sediments of fantasy. But, blast it, she was right. In a flash it began, the cascade of new life (you can chart it in our telephone bills) till, one day –

'Mum d'you think you really could? That'd be wonderful!'

There's a wistfulness about Sally, as if she's trying to remember a dream. Motherhood can do that to you. Your past peels away like those gantries you see crumbling down from a rocket that's about to be launched into space, but somehow the take-off never comes, you're more tied to earth than ever.

'It's a long way for you to drive in filthy weather –'

She hopes, knows, I'll contradict her.

'What time do you want me, darling?'

'Sally trusts me,' I explained to Brian.

'*Trusts* you! Why can't she trust a babysitter who lives a bit nearer? They'd have to pay then, wouldn't they, and oh dear they can't do that.'

I have to explain about Brian. He never had a grandfather. In his family they died early or ran off. So when he became one it was new territory for him. 'Of course, I'm delighted for Sally,' I heard him say; a sentence that seemed unfinished. Delight can sound chilling when the smile behind it's too flashful of teeth.

There was trouble brewing for him at work, I knew:

young stags pawing the ground, ready to lock antlers with the head of the herd. I'd met them at parties. 'I bet Brian's chuffed at being a grandfather!' Insincerity gleaming like flecks of champagne on cuff-linked sleeves.

I thought of that closed look and set jaw, the end-of-day uniform he'd been wearing recently.

'Won't you come too?' I asked, not because I mind driving the thirty miles to Sall's (it's a well-worn track) but because a pelting November evening's a sad setting for a night on your own.

'I'll be fine!' He rubbed his hands with naughtyboy glee: 'Got the rest of *Middlemarch* to watch!'

Here we go, true-or-false again . . . But after thirty years of marriage you don't ask, you know. You sense the signals as surely as a blind man reading braille, whatever way your face is turned.

Houses can glow as you drive away from them. As I backed the car out the rain was slithering the light from the windows into streaky squares while inside the TV flickered like shadows from an open fire.

Sall and Jeff's house was shuttered up, a dark blank in the tight-packed sloping row. I parked round the back and sploshed my way across their yard, feeling with my feet in case Rose's cart was on the path.

Jeff opened the door. I must have looked like a drowned rat.

'Didn't you bring an umbrella, Marge?' He has a way of saying things which makes you feel it's your fault. But I love him because he's Sally's choice and Rose's father. Those two things are enough for me.

'Sall's feeding her. She'll be down in a minute.'

I padded silently upstairs. Motherhood and grand motherhood have trained me to move like a ghost.

'Sall!' I breathed.

The room was lighted like a de la Tour canvas from a lamp on the floor. I almost expected to see Sall's fingers glow translucent red. Rose was suckling, eyes closed. Thirteen months and still at the breast.

Sall lifted her head. 'She's nearly asleep. She should be fine. Mum, thanks for coming!'

I didn't have to have it explained, didn't have to be told that otherwise she couldn't go out, that with me there she felt completely safe. It was the old biological thing again. Rose was my blood, Rose was part of me. That soft moleskin head hadn't quite come out of me, but nearly had.

The inert breathing lump, lips still bunched in their sucking shape, was lowered into the cot. Sall looped her breast into its bra and pulled down her shirt. She hooked in some silvery earrings.

'We'll be back about eleven. I've put your bedding downstairs, Mum.'

We went down together. There were a spoon and bowl on the table beside a pillbox tin of soup.

Sall hunched herself into her coat. 'Bye, Mum – and thanks!'

Jeff, last out of the door, echoed her. 'Bye, and thanks, Marge!'

He has a beautiful smile – when he wants to. Shut up, Marge, I thought. Rose would be a stunner, that's for sure.

Plenty to do. Washing up, fold nappies (no throw-aways for our Rose). The house felt chilly so after the soup I went into the sittingroom and lit the gas fire, which puttered cosily. The put-u-up was still in its sitting mode. I pulled it out, up-ended it and clicked it flat. Eleven would probably be more like twelve and I always prefer to be horizontal. Old age I find attacks the ankles first.

But I took a peep upstairs, leaning into that aromatic

nest. A breath of baby a day keeps the doctor away . . .

The ring of the phone went through me like an electric shock. Stumble downstairs –

'Hullo!'

'Marge, you all right?'

'Brian!' Oh Brian, did you have to –

'I thought I'd just check everything was okay. Done your breastfeeding, cooked their meals for the next three weeks?'

'*Brian* . . .' I took a deep breath. 'How was *Middlemarch?*'

'It ended with her marrying that young chap. It's strange –' he sounded really puzzled. 'Do you think that's plausible, do women really go for younger men?'

'Oh Brian.' My shoeless feet ached as shafts of cold air flowed across the floor. 'This woman just wants to put some slippers on – which she's forgotten to bring – and crawl into bed with a hot water bottle.'

'Pity I'm not there.'

'Yes!' Marriage had its uses, after all.

'Well, I'll let you go. Don't do too much. They've got to learn to stand on their own feet one day.'

He's thinking about that loan (loan? gift) for the car. But what are young people to do these days?

The gas fire had turned the front room into an oven. I de-gelled my feet, stopped my face from scorching with a magazine – a paperback wasn't big enough. Then heat induced somnalence . . . Hunt for my bag, get ready to curl into bed, no need of a hot bottle – ah!

Stretch legs, wriggle toes against the duvet (which smells of my last visit) and look around the room at the life my children have created in their little matchbox house.

There are things I recognise, from our shared past, things I don't. Pictures, plants, colours, shapes, a whole life that's theirs but also familiar, as if places – houses, rooms –

have a heredity you can map, as well as people. But the noises outside are strange; car doors slamming, the sudden crescendo of talk on clip-clop heels along the street, the –

'Waaa!'

I shoot up in bed. Wait. Maybe she's only having a dream –

'Waaaa! Mmmm-a!'

Oh hell. What should I do? take up a bottle, a dummy? She must be full to the brim –

'Waaaaaaaaaa!'

Dummy, dummy, where are you . . . Coming my love! – no, don't call, pretend to be Sall. Skim upstairs –

Pat, gently, firmly ('When she wakes at night I just pat her back to sleep'). Here's the dummy –

'Waaaaa! Mmmm-aaa!'

Pat, pat . . .

A head rears up like an angry cannonball: 'Waaa!'

Jesus, what do I do? Mama coming SOON ('she recognises lots of words' – but I bet that's not one of them), oh you little terror, oh my sweet.

I do the only thing I can: pick up the sobbing bundle, fold it into my arms.

She smells of tears and acrid baby sweat . . . and suddenly jerks away from me. Dark eyes pinion mine. I'm being interrogated: *how can you explain your presence here?*

'All right, my darling,' this time I speak out loud. 'You're coming downstairs with me.'

I have to wake her up completely. Turn night, when I'm a stranger, into day, when I'm the loved and loving gran.

There's a kind of drunkenness about a sleepless child. Rose takes the dummy, sucks on its empty teat, stares black-eyed in manic concentration as I flick my way through Peter Rabbit/Tom Kitten/Jeremy Fisher, anything I can find until they become a long kittenfrograbbit sausage of shiny pages with soggy fingers stabbed at them.

'Mor-mm-mm!'

So, on to the eternal wheel of nursery rhymes. Tom Tom the piper's son, Lavender's blue . . . and the fire splutters and fills the room with heat.

As her cheeks grow redder I lean across and turn out the furious opal flames; breathe cooler, hitch her back into my lap – and zonk, she's fallen asleep like a stone.

The curling curtains of her eyelids are still beaded with, not tears but the moisture of contained distress. Her cheeks have little pits where the colour concentrates.

I brush my lips against her forehead, inhale that scented mouse bouquet. I think, my darling Rose, I love you more than all the world.

And as she settles into sleep my arm begins to ache as if it's a sack of cement I'm cradling.

The sound of a key turning in the latch comes into the edges of my dream – which is about going somewhere and not having the key or is it the wrong one – and I'm dreaming it at the same time as I know it's real, which involves a funny kind of swimming up into myself or (in this case) . . . fear.

Door closing, very quietly. Soft footsteps.

('*Grandmother and baby found –*')

'Brian!' My heart is galloping.

'I brought you these.'

For a split second I see him as a stranger. Large, untidy, with an ancient sweater over suit trousers and the look of a man who's left home without thinking what kind of weather's going on outside. He's holding a plastic bag like an offering.

I motion with my head; at sleeping Rose. And suddenly see myself with his eyes, caught in that defensive grand-maternal pose: hands off, baby first!

'What's she doing here?'

I don't say 'Shsh', though it wells up.

'What are *you* doing here?'

'Bringing your slippers.'

'My slippers!'

'You said you were cold. On the phone.'

I'm caught between laughter and something closer to tears. A lie has to be strong to carry the weight of such transparency. And this is a weak lie.

Brian has come for company. He's driven thirty miles – in his slippers, for god's sake – because he doesn't want to be alone. Not just now.

Children sleep through the noise of thunder and revving cars. But whispers can wake them up.

'Waaaa – !'

Her eyes are still closed. That square of mouth does all the seeing she needs.

'Put her to bed, Marge, do!'

'Sweetheart, Mummy'll be back *soon!*'

Our words converge, swords that are used to clashing.

Then, 'Ouf, she doesn't half stink!'

'Rose!'

'You think even her shit smells of ambrosia? Oh, my poor besotted Marge!'

'In that case,' I look levelly at him, 'why don't *you* fetch the nappies and change her . . . while I make tea.'

'Hullo – can we join the party?'

Giggling, Sall flumps down on a cushion. Jeff, amazed, hovers by the door. They've still got on their outdoor things and what with scarves and coats and the tea cups and bedding and nappies and Rose it's quite a crowd.

And Brian, too. Particularly Brian, who always seems so large in any small space. Brian sits on the bed like someone in a waiting room, knees drawn up, luggage on his lap.

But his luggage is – Rose.

A new face, new outline, new touch, new voice? How can one tell. It'd worked. He had laid her down on the put-u-up and she gazed at him in goggle-eyed surprise. 'Here you are, young lady!' He lifted her legs like someone degutting a chicken. 'My goodness, we are in a mess.' And I became the au pair or plumber's mate. 'Cotton wool, please,' then 'more cotton wool'. And a clean Rose had finally lain there, gurgling her gratitude.

In the discomfort of a bed meant to be for two but really for one, Brian held me in his arms.

'Are you reliving your past, my love?'

'Heaven forbid!'

'Then what is it – why this fanatical devotion?'

'Because,' I took a long breath; because they need it, because this is the most difficult moment in any couple's life . . . and heard myself say, 'As I get older the past seems to evaporate, the present is all I've got. And it's intertwined with Rose's, totally, as if there's a golden net cast between her and me. Just for a while I want to do this thing properly, accept it for the blessing it is and not look beyond. Like Rose – live in the present. You see, I'm learning from her!'

'While I,' he stopped. After a short pause, 'The future is what I think about the whole time,' he said.

'Let's swap roles –'

'We'll see.'

'Future again,' I murmured.

I felt for his hands. Among the jumble of our limbs under the flopping duvet I searched for them and found them. And netted them in mine.

AUTHOR NOT KNOWN
One Immortality

This poem is believed to have been written between the wars.

I often think that women who first hold
A grandchild in their arms, must feel that hour
Is one of life's supremest. Growing old
Is now for ever robbed of half its power,
The threat of age has surely lost its sting.
For in their children's children they become
A part of life's perpetual blossoming.
And when their strength grows less, their senses numb,
Beneath the frost of age, they realise
New life is growing fed from their own veins.
The dreams they lost begin once more to rise
In fresh young lives; a newer vision reigns.
They know the stream of life flows strong and free,
And feel a part of immortality.

The Fragrance of Herbs

In this fictionalised account of a boy's relationship with his grandfather, Jayabrato Chatterjee, who lives in Calcutta, draws on his own childhood and memories of staying with his grandparents in the north of India.

Dadubhai was Roy's paternal grandfather and his Bhagvad Gita, bursting at the spine, had fascinating pictures. They related mainly to wars and battles, as severed heads pierced by arrows flew across a fiery sky. The holy book lay at the invisible feet of a black blob of stone, the most venerable Narayansheela, who was rather dull and chipped.

In Dadubhai's retreat there was a special corner for many gods and goddesses, imprisoned behind glass barriers and ornate wooden frames. Some hung from the wall and some stood propped around Mr Narayansheela. Lakshmi sat on a pink lotus and Saraswati rode a white swan, playing an enormous veena. Kali drooled her tongue and rolled her eyes and danced on Shiva's chest. Kartik almost whipped a comb out from his pocket, ready to frisk it through his hippy locks. Ganesh looked woebegone and didn't know where to place his curly trunk. Vishnu sprouted a lotus poised on a long stem from his belly button. The entire coterie sported a film of dust that powdered their benign, superior smiles. They weren't very bothered by cockroaches running up and down their bodies.

Only Mr Narayansheela lounged on a flower-bedecked silver throne that needed polishing badly. His non-existent face was smothered with sandalwood paste and around his dais were tiny copper plates containing his calorie-rich diet of sliced fruit and a heap of sugar, infested with scurrying red ants. His drinking water was poured into a small tumbler from Dadubhai's pitcher. The paraphernalia of cutlery and a starched napkin were happily dispensed with. And Mr Narayansheela found no earthly use for finger bowls because he had no hands!

Once morning prayers and mantras were recited, Kanchiama came to clear plates and replenish the diet, depending on how much the gods and cockroaches had gobbled. If plates were badly soiled, she took them away and washed them with a mixture of ash, tamarind and blind devotion till they gleamed and sparkled. Only five days in the month Janak Thakur took this task over. Roy pestered his ayah to find out why she couldn't wash up for Mr Narayansheela every single day when she did it happily for the rest of the family. Kanchiama cuffed his head and snickered but gave no answers. And Roy became apprehensive for the first time and didn't run to get a response from Laldida.

He often sat cross-legged on the floor, facing Mr Narayansheela and his celestial cronies, and listened to Dadubhai recite prayers. After each verse the old man rang the brass bell with a slender stem that ended up becoming the magic head of Serpent Kalia. The bell lay near the dais and invariably, when it was lifted, a baby cockroach scuttled from its shelter. Dadubhai lit incense and Kanchiama brought in fresh flowers in a small wicker basket and decorated Mr Narayansheela's throne. Once in a while Roy recited along with Dadubhai, Sanskrit shlokas, both incong-ruous and comforting, in a lilting, pedantic cadence:

Gurur Brahma Gurur Vishnu
Gurur Devo Maheshwara
Gurur Sakshaat Parabrahma
Tasmy Shri Guruvey Namah!

Our teacher's Brahma! Our teacher's Vishnu! He's the God of Gods, Maheshwara! O Supreme Master, our Ultimate Reality, to you we bow our heads!

But Fussy Farida, Roy's classteacher, was a woman! She wore butterflies in her hair but no lotuses and water lilies bloomed from her navel! And as for the games-master, Butlerwhite, well, the less said about that silly Anglo-Indian the better! Butlerwhite was no Brahma: with his blue eyes, walrus moustache and a whistle dangling around his neck! Could Ma Mannering, the Headmistress, with the dreadful malacca, ever hope to be the Ultimate Reality?

Certainly not!

Then what was Dadubhai's prayer all about ? What was this blessed Ultimate Reality? Who knew the answers? Why did the north wind charge down the mountains and toss petals, full-blown, into Meerama's rose-bowl? Why did Kanchiama light an earthen lamp at the feet of the tulsi plant every evening and let the breeze snuff it out? In the fading twilight, why did drops of water quiver on lotus leaves in the lily pond and look glorious and fragile?

Roy loved Dadubhai. He loved his silver locks and his serene wrinkled face. And he loved the pungent odour of Chavanprash and the fragrance of herbs emitting from his mouth. His eyes watered if he sat too long at his prayers. The sagging skin made small criss-crosses on his upper arms and he had a stock of fabulous stories up his crumpled fatua sleeves. Only when Roy came to spend time with him in the retreat did Dadubhai give him a handful of peppermint lozenges and unfold his tales, killing stray bugs that spluttered blood on his sheets the colour of catechu in spicy paans.

Roy didn't much care for the picture of Lord Yama he saw in Dadubhai's stack of fat prayer books. Uncertainly, he peered at the dark visage of the King of Death and asked, 'Will he take you away as well, Dadubhai?'

'Oh yes,' Dadubhai replied. 'He spares no mortal.'

'Then why can't people become immortal?'

'Some great men do. With their thoughts and deeds. We read about them in books or see paintings by them in museums and get inspired.'

'Will Meerama become immortal, Dadubhai? Will people become inspired by her canvases too?'

Dadubhai stared at his grandson, stroked his beard but made no reply. His rheumy eyes were expressionless and remained as stubborn as Yama's.

'Will Yama come and take Ruth Zacharia away?' Roy questioned, unsure if she hadn't already met him at her three-legged seance table.

Dadubhai ruffled his hair and said, 'Yes he will. No one's spared. Not even Ruth Zacharia!'

'That's not true,' Roy retorted. 'He let Savitri off. Don't you remember the story you told me? About how Savitri chased Yama and brought back her dead husband, Satyavan, to earth?'

'Hers was an exceptional case!' Dadubhai chuckled.

'So you'll die one day?'

'Yes, that's as sure as every new morning. But who knows, I may be born again!'

'Dadubhai, please, please pray hard so that you're born again as my best friend!'

'I'm already your friend, aren't I?'

'Yes you are. But then there's such a difference being somebody's best friend and just an ordinary pal!'

'All right child. I'll pray hard and hope your wish comes true!'

Roy smiled at Dadubhai, satisfied, and proceeded to

discuss more serious business. He said, pensively, 'Dadubhai, when you die, will you leave behind your prayer bell for me?'

'Just the prayer bell?'

'And your spectacles, if you don't mind.'

'What will you do with my spectacles and the prayer bell, child?'

'Why, I'll take them to school of course! I'll wear your glasses so I can spot enemies from a mile and ring the bell hard if bullies from other dorms come to harass my friends!'

Dadubhai was amused. He promised Roy his spectacles and the prayer bell with the head of Kalia, once the King of Death carried him away on the back of his rapacious bull, beyond the horizon and across still waters of the Vaikunth River every man was doomed to pass.

PO CHÜ-I (772–846)

Last Poem

Po Chü-I was a major poet of the T'ang Dynasty in China. He held high office in the imperial administration but was later demoted. He consoled himself by building a retreat and writing poetry, which he also used as a mode of communication with his companions. (Translation by Arthur Waley.)

They have put my bed beside the unpainted screen;
They have shifted my stove in front of the blue curtain.
I listen to my grandchild reading me a book;
I watch the servants, heating up my soup.
With rapid pencil I answer the poems of friends,
I feel in my pockets and pull out medicine-money.
When this superintendence of trifing affairs is done,
I lie back on my pillows and sleep with my face to the
  south.

Acknowledgements

Permission to reproduce stories and poems by the following authors is gratefully acknowledged:

Marcel Proust: to Random House UK Ltd for the extract from *Remembrance of Things Past*. Copyright © Chatto & Windus and Random House 1981

Leo Tolstoy: to Rosemary Edmonds and Penguin Books Ltd for the extract from *Childhood, Boyhood, Youth* translated by Rosemary Edmonds, Penguin Classics 1964. Copyright © Rosemary Edmonds 1964

David Malouf: to Random House UK Ltd for 'At My Grandmother's' from *Selected Poems 1959-89*, Chatto & Windus, 1994. Copyright © David Malouf

Isaac Babel: to David McDuff and Penguin Books Ltd for the extract from *Collected Stories* translated by David McDuff, Penguin Books 1994. Copyright © David McDuff 1994

Bertrand Russell: to Routledge and the Bertrand Russell Peace Foundation for the extract from *The Autobiography of Bertrand Russell*, Allen & Unwin 1967. Copyright © George Allen & Unwin 1967

Doris Lessing: to the author and Jonathan Clowes for 'Flight' from *The Habit of Loving*, MacGibbon & Kee 1957. Reprinted by permission of Jonathan Clowes on behalf of Doris Lessing. Copyright © Doris Lessing

John Storton: to the author for 'A Grandad's Wishes'. Copyright © John Storton

John Galsworthy: to the Society of Authors as the literary representatives of the Estate of John Galsworthy for the

extract from *The Forsyte Saga*. Copyright © The Estate of
John Galsworthy

Dylan Thomas: to J M Dent and David Higham Associates
Ltd for 'A Visit to Grandpa's' from *Portrait of the Artist as a
Young Dog*, J M Dent 1940. Copyright © Trustees of the late
Dylan Thomas

Queen Victoria: to Richard Hough, William Heinemann
Ltd and Reed Consumer Books Ltd for the extracts from
*Advice to a Granddaughter – letters from Queen Victoria to
Princess Victoria of Hesse* edited by Richard Hough, William
Heinemann 1975. Copyright © Richard Hough 1975

Margaret Walker: to the author for 'Lineage' from *For My
People*, Yale University Press 1942. Copyright © Margaret
Walker

Kathleen Dayus: to Virago Press Ltd for the extract from
Her People, Virago Press 1982. Copyright © Kathleen Dayus
1982

Jung Chang: to the author and HarperCollins Publishers
Ltd for the extract from *Wild Swans*, Flamingo 1993.
Copyright © Globalfair 1991

Diana Holman Hunt: to the author and Peters Frazer &
Dunlop for the extract from *My Grandmothers and I*,
Hamish Hamilton 1960. Copyright © Diana Holman Hunt
1960

Grace Nichols: to Virago Press Ltd for 'Granny Granny
Please Comb My Hair' from *Lazy Thoughts of a Lazy
Woman*, Virago Press 1989. Copyright © Grace Nichols
1989

Sylvia Townsend Walker: to Susanna Pinney, William
Maxwell and *The New Yorker* for the extract from *The
Children's Grandmother*, published in *The New Yorker* 1950.
Copyright © Susanna Pinney and William Maxwell

Walter de la Mare: to the Literary Trustees of Walter de la Mare and the Society of Authors as their representatives for 'The Cupboard' from *The Complete Poems of Walter de la Mare*, Faber & Faber 1969. Copyright © The Literary Trustees of Walter de la Mare

Marjorie Shostak: reprinted by permission of the publishers from *Nisa: The Life and Words of a !Kung Woman* by Marjorie Shostak, Cambridge, Mass, Harvard University Press 1981. Copyright © Marjorie Shostak 1981

Salim Hakim: to the author for the extract from *Grandma and I*, published for the first time in this collection. Copyright © Salim Hakim 1995

Helena Norberg-Hodge: to Random House UK Ltd for the extract from *Ancient Futures: Learning from Ladakh*, Rider 1992. Copyright © Helena Norberg-Hodge 1991

Daphne Glazer: to the author for 'Phoenix Rising', published for the first time in this collection and broadcast on BBC Radio 4 on 23 May 1995. Copyright © Daphne Glazer 1995

Nell Dunn: to Random House UK Ltd for the extract from *Grandmothers*, Jonathan Cape 1991. Copyright © Nell Dunn 1991

Elizabeth Cairns: to the author for 'Milestones', published for the first time in this collection. Copyright © Elizabeth Cairns 1995

Jayabrato Chatterjee: to the author for 'The Fragrance of Herbs' from *The Last Train to Innocence*. Copyright © Jayabrato Chatterjee

Maxim Gorky: the extract from *My Childhood* is taken from the edition published by Elek in 1953.

Tom Sayachapis: 'Advice to his Grandson' is taken from Ruth Kirk, *Wisdom of the Elders*, Douglas & MacIntyre, 1986.

Every effort has been made to trace copyright holders in all copyright material in this book. The editor regrets if there has been any oversight and suggests the publisher is contacted in any such event.